Copper Trails and Iron Rails
More Voyages into Michigan's Past

An irate subscriber to Thomas A. Edison's gossipy newspaper pitches the young author into the St. Clair River.

Copper Trails and Iron Rails
More Voyages into Michigan's Past

By Larry B. Massie

Avery Color Studios
Au Train, Michigan
1989

Copyright 1989
by Larry B. Massie
and
Avery Color Studios

Library of Congress Card No. 89-83953
ISBN-0-932212-60-3
First Edition—May 1989
Reprinted—1989, 1990, 1993

Cover by Diane Tedora

Published by Avery Color Studios
Marquette, Michigan 49855

Printed in Michigan, U.S.A. by
Lake Superior Press
Marquette, Michigan 49855

Dedication

In memory of George Wiskemann (May 24, 1904-October 19, 1988), collector, historian and friend, whose zest for life will always be an inspiration.

TABLE OF CONTENTS

Foreword

Where is Michigan? That is easy enough to answer --
merely get out an atlas. What is Michigan? Here is a
more difficult question. Most people, I suspect think of
automobiles and the companies that make them, of
Battle Creek and breakfast cereals, of Detroit Tigers,
Lions, Red Wings, and Pistons, of Michigan University
and Michigan State and their football and basketball
teams, and of cold and snow. If they happen to be
acquainted with American history, then perhaps they
also remember that Michigan had something to do with
the War of 1812, that Henry and Gerald Ford lived there,
and that it produced several would-be presidents who
never quite made it, such as Lewis Cass and Arthur
Vandenberg. Otherwise their knowledge -- and this
tends to be true of residents as well as outsiders --
contains only a few other such odds and ends. Indeed, it
is quite possible they believe that Michigan does not have
a history, or if it does, it is a dull one.

Certainly that was my attitude when, a native of
Kansas, I came to this state almost thirty years ago.
Since then I have learned differently. Moreover, no one
has contributed more to my education along this line
than the author of this book, Larry Massie. Larry is a
former student of mine -- an excellent one, I will add.
Starting in January 1987 I have been his student. That is
when he began publishing a weekly article on Michigan
history in the *Kalamazoo Gazette* and the other Booth
newspapers of the state. Along with thousands of other
readers I have discovered that Michigan has a colorfully
kaleidoscopic history consisting of red men, blacks, and
whites, of women and men and some sort of in-between,

11

of murderers and martyrs, explorers and lost towns, poets and politicians, rogues and heroes, and of fish, birds, and buffaloes, all spanning a time that ranges from the primeval to the present. Some of the people and things Larry writes about are famous, others he has retrieved from the depths of obscurity, but all are fascinating.

Fascinating too is the way in which he tells their stories. Aware that if history seems dull, it probably is the fault of the historian and not the history, he writes so that the reader can enjoy the pleasure of reading along with the pleasure of learning. Yet he does not sacrifice accuracy to entertainment. He makes every effort to get at the facts and present them objectively. This is all that any historian can do, and Larry does it very well.

Those of you who have had the opportunity to read Larry's articles as they appeared, or who have read the first collection of them, *Voyages into Michigan's Past*, published in 1988, already know the truth of what is stated above. Those of you who have not can now find this out for yourselves -- and in the process get a lot of answers to the question: What is Michigan?

Albert Castel
Western Michigan University

Preface

"All Aboard!" and welcome to another series of Voyages Into Michigan's Past. Once again we'll tour the length and breadth of our great state. We'll visit 17th century Sault Ste. Marie, 18th century Detroit, 19th century Singapore before it was swallowed up by sand dunes, and in the 20th century we'll hop on a buckboard with Booker T. Washington for a jaunt through the famous black settlement in Cass County.

I have booked passage for you on the Griffin, the Walk-in-the-Water and the ill-fated Alpena. We'll take a ride in a "Merry Oldsmobile," peddle one of Warren Sheffield's velocipedes down the track and board the Erie and Kalamazoo Railroad. Watch out for "snake heads!"

Along the way it will be my pleasure to introduce you to some remarkable Michiganders, including young Thomas Edison; little Willie Filley, the lost Jackson boy, and that perennial 14-year-old, Charlie McCarthy, the "magnificent splinter." You'll meet Will Carleton, a pretty good poet, and Julia Moore, a pretty bad one; athletes Joe Louis and "Hurry-up" Yost; Civil War soldiers Robert Hendershot, the drummer boy of the Rappahannock, and Pvt. Franklin Thompson, a he who was a she. I've lined up a contingent of colorful medics: Ann Arbor's Dr. Chase, Dr. Kellogg of Battle Creek, Dr. Protar, Beaver Island's "heaven-sent friend," and Dr. Peebles, whose practice included this world as well as the next. Hold onto your wallets when you're in the company of badman Sile Doty or the bank-robbing Bidwell brothers.

After you've taken this pilgrimage into Michigan's

past, I hope you'll agree with me that whatever you call these fellow Wolverines, it won't be boring. I encourage you to explore in greater detail these historical vignettes by consulting the sources listed in the bibliography.

The 52 essays in this collection originally appeared in the Kalamazoo Gazette, Grand Rapids Press, Muskegon Chronicle, Jackson Citizen-Patriot, Ann Arbor News, Saginaw News and Bay City Times. I thank the publishers and editors of those Booth newspapers for recognizing that the public's interest in Michigan history extends well beyond the sesquicentennial celebration of 1987.

Jim Mosby, editor of the Kalamazoo Gazette, and Mary Kramer, metro-editor of the Kalamazoo Gazette, have been particularly supportive. I have been fortunate in having available the masterful editing services of Dave Person of the Kalamazoo Gazette. As usual, my wife, friend and partner, Priscilla, provided me with inspiration as well as word processing and skilled copystand work. Al Beet of Allegan worked well into the wee hours on several occasions to produce unparalleled photographic processing. Dr. Le Roy Barnett, reference archivist at the State of Michigan Archives, generously shared his valuable research.

Again, my special thanks go to the many newspaper readers who encouraged me to continue this series.

Larry B. Massie
Allegan Forest

The Pageant
of the Sault

Father Claude Dablon begins the "Pageant of the Sault" in 1671.

With a hollow thump audible even above the roar of the St. Marys rapids, the base of the huge cedar cross slid into the hole that had been dug to receive it. Arms upraised, Father Claude Dablon sanctified the cross with a Latin prayer. Then the party of Frenchmen assembled on the hill near the Jesuit mission at Sault Ste. Marie doffed their chapeaus and sang an ancient hymn.

Vexilla Regis proderunt
Fulget crucis mysterium

Seated in a semicircle, the chiefs of the 14 tribes who had been summoned from a radius of 500 miles, and behind them some 2,000 of their people, solemnly watched the white man's ritual. It was June 14, 1671, and the monumental event that has come to be known as the "Pageant of the Sault" was about to commence.

Jean Talon, who as intendant was responsible to report to the king on the activities of the governor and the bishop of New France, had conceived the idea of the pageant following a visit to the court of Louis XIV. The ceremony would legitimize French claims to the interior of the North American continent, thereby hemming in the British colonies east of the Appalachians and thwarting the fur trading encroachments of the newly formed Hudson's Bay Company. It would also cement French authority over the northern tribes.

Talon selected Sieur de St. Lusson, a French soldier of fortune who had traveled from France to Canada in the same vessel with him, to head up the expedition. St. Lusson, in company with Nicolas Perrot, a 26-year-old voyageur who served as interpreter, explorer Louis Joliet, and 15 other soldiers and fur traders, set out from Montreal in the fall of 1670. Owing to the lateness of the season, they wintered over at the Manitoulin Islands.

Early the following spring, Perrot and other emissaries visited the various northern tribes, inviting representatives to attend the ceremony to be held at strategically located Sault Ste. Marie. The Indians received the French with traditional hospitality. At Green Bay, local tribesmen staged a sham battle and a game of lacrosse for their entertainment.

When Perrot and a party of Sacs, Winnebagos and Menominees reached the Sault on May 5, 1671, they found St. Lusson and his men already there. The wigwams of other Indian delegates stretched along the river bank at the foot of the rapids.

On June 14, a procession of French soldiers in full dress uniform and black-robed Jesuit priests Father Dablon, Gabriel Druillette, Claude Allouez and Louis Andre marched from the mission stockade to the brow of a hill near the present site of the lighted fountain in the government park. After the planting of the cedar cross, a metal plate engraved with the royal arms of France was attached to another cedar post. Then St. Lusson stepped forward, a glittering sword in one hand and in the other a tuft of sod, proclaiming three times in a loud voice the annexation by Louis XIV of all lands "which have been discovered and those which may be discovered hereafter, in all their length and breadth, bounded on the one side by the seas of the north and west and on the other side by the South Sea." In other words, France had just claimed practically the entire North American continent.

The French soldiers fired their muskets and shouted "Long live the King" in triumph, and the Indians joined in with whooping and dancing, little realizing that they were celebrating the loss of their domain. When the tumult died down, Father Allouez delivered a speech intended to impress upon the Indians the power of their new king.

"When he attacks, he is more terrible than the thunder: the earth trembles, the air and the sea are set on fire by the discharge of his cannon; while he has been seen amid his squadrons, all covered with the blood of his

17

foes, of whom he has slain so many with his sword that he does not count their scalps, but the rivers of blood that he sets flowing."

Allouez continued with a description of the king's wealth. "You count yourself rich when you have ten or twelve sacks of corn, some hatchets, glass beads, kettles, or other things of that sort. He has towns of his own, more in number than you have people in all these countries five hundred leagues around; while in each town there are warehouses containing enough hatchets to cut down all your forest, kettles to cook all your moose, and glass beads to fill all your cabins."

Following Allouez's harangue, St. Lusson gave a stirring martial oration translated by Perrot. Then 20 French soldiers and fur traders signed a document acknowledging the proceedings. That evening a huge bonfire, in lieu of fireworks, terminated the pageant.

The next day, St. Lusson and party left for a short tour of Lake Superior. Upon his return to the Sault, he was dismayed to find the cedar pole and the metallic royal escutcheon missing. He never learned exactly what became of it. Probably it was made of lead and was cast into bullets by the local Indians.

The cedar cross enjoyed a longer existence. It stood for generations, and as late as the 19th century had become part of the oral tradition of descendants of the original spectators of the Pageant of the Sault.

France lost the North American empire it claimed in 1671 to Britain during the French and Indian War nearly a century later. The British maintained control of the territory that ultimately became Michigan until 1796. But it was the Americans, who, in the process of carving a state out of the wilderness, demonstrated the prophetic nature of Allouez's claims of the powers of his French king.

The Voyage of the Griffin

THE " GRIFFIN."

The Griffin, the first ship to ply lakes Erie, Huron and Michigan.

Eyes tearing in the sharp December wind, Sieur de La Salle started into the Lake Michigan horizon from atop a high bluff at the mouth of the St. Joseph River. It was December 3, 1679, and for over a month La Salle had moodily scanned the lake for the distant sails of the Griffin, the first ship to ply lakes Erie, Huron and Michigan. While they waited, he and his men had erected a 40-foot by 80-foot palisaded fort they called Miami after their name for the St. Joseph River.

Four months before, Robert Cavelier, Sieur de La Salle, a protege of Count Frontenac, governor of New France, had embarked on a threefold mission. He intended to exploit Lake Michigan's rich fur trade, to explore the Mississippi Valley in hopes of finding a water route to the Gulf of Mexico, and to establish a chain of forts from Canada southward that would insure French dominion over the interior of the continent.

La Salle had dispatched an advance party of 15 fur traders to Lake Michigan during the fall of 1678. The following January, another work force under command of his trusty lieutenant, Henry Tonty, had established a shipyard above Niagara Falls just west of the mouth of Cayuga Creek. Tonty, who had amputated his own hand after a grenade had mangled it during a naval engagement, possessed a will as strong as the iron hand he had adopted in its stead. His habit of thumping the heads of Indians with his iron hand when angry earned from them a healthy respect.

By August, Tonty's shipbuilders had completed a 45- to 60-ton sailing vessel sporting a mythological griffin on its prow in honor of Frontenac's coat of arms. Men on shore helped tow it upstream, and the Griffin sailed out into Lake Erie on August 7. It carried 32 passengers, including Louis Hennepin, a 37-year-old Recollet friar who would later immortalize the voyage in an exciting if not wholly trustworthy account published in 1683.

The Griffin enjoyed three days of smooth sailing to the

mouth of the Detroit River. Some trouble was experienced in sounding a passage through the St. Clair Flats, so named by Hennepin because the day marked the festival of Sainte Claire. Proceeding along the west coast of Lake Huron, the ship encountered a violent tempest somewhere off Thunder Bay. As the ship pitched at the mercy of the waves, everyone fell on their knees for a lengthy prayer, except for the pilot, that is, a veteran sailor who "did nothing all that while but curse and swear against M. La Salle, who he said had brought him thither to make him perish in a nasty lake, and lose the glory he had acquired by his long and happy navigations on the ocean."

Despite the pilot's profuse imprecations, the vessel survived the storm. On August 27, the Griffin cast anchor at St. Ignace, astonishing the local Indians with a salute from its seven iron cannons. There, La Salle learned that some of the men he had sent ahead the preceeding fall had deserted, absconding with a quantity of his supplies to Sault Ste. Marie. He sent Tonty to the Sault in pursuit and owing to the lateness of the season, La Salle sailed ahead into Green Bay.

At Washington Island he found more of his advance party. They had assembled a choice cache of furs. Contrary to the counsel of his men, La Salle, who, according to Hennepin, "never took any one's advice," sent the Griffin loaded with the furs back to Niagara Falls, following which it was to return to the Straits of Mackinac for directions to a yet undetermined rendezvous point.

La Salle watched the Griffin sail into the distance on September 18. It would be the last he would ever see of his vessel. The exact fate of the Griffin will never be fully known, but according to some Indians, the Griffin had anchored briefly somewhere along the north shore of Lake Michigan. They had warned the pilot of an impending storm, but the salty old sailor ventured out anyway, to vanish from sight amid the huge whitecaps of a howling gale.

In the meantime, La Salle and 14 of his followers in four canoes paddled south along the west coast of Lake Michigan. They narrowly escaped the same storm that presumedly took the Griffin. Rounding the tip of the lake, at the present site of Chicago, they landed at the mouth of the St. Joseph on November 1.

After he had captured the deserters at the Sault, Tonty traveled down the east side of the lake to join La Salle on November 20. Realizing that the Griffin had probably been lost, La Salle nevertheless determined to continue on his mission. On December 3, he and 30 men in eight canoes paddled up the St. Joseph River to the Kankakee Portage near the present site of South Bend, Indiana.

After many hardships, La Salle arrived at the present site of Peoria, Illinois on January 5, 1680. There he constructed Fort Crevecoeur, "the first fixed establishment built by white men in the entire Mississippi Valley." His men also cut the timbers for another vessel which he intended to sail down the Mississippi. But he lacked the ironwork and rigging the Griffin was to supply.

In early March he set out on a return journey to secure that equipment. He arrived back at Fort Miami on March 24, built a raft to pole up the St. Joseph as far as possible and then became the first white man to traverse southern Michigan. La Salle's incredible journey to Montreal took 65 days in all.

La Salle returned to Fort Miami late in 1681 and proceeded to successfully navigate the length of the Mississippi. On April 9, 1682, at the Gulf of Mexico, La Salle planted a cross bearing the arms of France and claimed for his king the entire Mississippi Valley. Following several other adventurous explorations, La Salle was murdered by his own mutinous men somewhere on the Brazos River in Texas on March 19, 1687.

Michigan's Mysterious "Garden Beds"

A rare photograph of Indian garden beds taken before they disappeared forever.

The pioneers called them "garden beds" because they resembled the formal flower gardens wealthy horticulturalists once laid out on their estates. Who constructed them and why, not even the native Ottawa and Potawatomi knew. And since all traces of the mysterious earthworks that once dotted southern Michigan prairies have been obliterated, we probably never will know.

The French explorer M. Varennes de la Verenderye, who in 1731 became the first European to cross the continent to the Rocky Mountains, marveled at "large tracts free from wood many of which were everywhere covered with furrows, as if they had formerly been ploughed and sown."

The pioneers who streamed into Michigan a century later discovered tracts as large as 300 acres covered with the strange furrows. Some sites lay as far north as Saginaw County but the beds were most prevalent in the Grand, St. Joseph and Kalamazoo river valleys.

Most garden beds consisted of raised parallel ridges of earth, from five to 14 feet in width and from 12 to 30 feet long, arranged in a series of plats at right angles to each other. Sunken paths, six to 18 inches below the surface of the ground, divided the rows. Seven other types have been described, however, ranging from fanciful geometric designs to wheel-like spokes radiating out from a raised hub.

Regardless of their shape, the beds were invariably located on prairies or park-like "oak openings" where the soil was the most fertile. The indigenous vegetation, thickly matted prairie grass, apparently preserved their form for centuries. Another common characteristic was the absence of stone artifacts usually found in conjunction with mounds and other prehistoric earthworks.

In 1827, the Reverend Isaac McCoy, who had established a Baptist Indian mission at the present site of

Grand Rapids, cut down a huge oak tree growing atop a nearby set of garden beds. He counted 325 annual growth rings on the stump, indicating that set of beds had been abandoned before 1502.

John T. Blois' immigrants' guide to Michigan published in 1838 included a section on garden beds. Blois described a notable group of beds covering 100 acres located on the west bank of the St. Joseph River near present-day Three Rivers. "It is to be hoped," he urged, "that some exertions will be made by the scientific, to rescue these ancient relics from an oblivion, to which the otherwise absorbing business of an enterprising people, or the ignorance or heedless inadvertence of others may subject them."

The garden beds might have stood a chance of survival had they not been located on the best agricultural land. But the prairies and oak openings were the first to be taken up by settlers, and within a few decades ox-drawn plows had erased what had resisted centuries of time and the elements.

In Kalamazoo, for example, early settlers found a system of garden beds, including several of the rare wheel-shaped variety up to 90 feet in diameter, covering a ten-acre plat south of the famous Indian mound in Bronson Park. That mound owes its survival to the fact that it happened to lie on land reserved for public use by village founder Titus Bronson. The garden beds, however, soon became the first of Kalamazoo's historic sites to fall prey to urban development.

Volney Hascall, an early editor of the *Kalamazoo Gazette*, recalled a similar mound and circular garden bed located four miles south of Kalamazoo on the farm his family settled on in 1831. Kalamazoo County, in fact, once boasted at least 22 garden beds, more than any other county in Michigan or Wisconsin, the only states where such earthworks have been positively identified.

J.R. Cumings remembered plowing up a set of garden

beds located in Comstock Township. The ridges were so high that every time he crossed a dividing path the plow share came entirely out of the earth. J.T. Cobb, on the other hand, took great pains to preserve as a monument a portion of the fine examples that lay on his farm near Schoolcraft. Unfortunately in 1864, the roots of the protective prairie grass were "eaten off by white grubs, and the hogs, in search of mischief-makers, caused the utter destruction of the beds by rooting them up."

Whether or not they fell to hogs, four-footed or biped, by 1877 when antiquarian researcher Bela Hubbard of Detroit investigated the garden beds he found "nearly every trace has disappeared." His scholarly efforts had been preceded by those of Michigan's most celebrated ethnologist, Henry Rowe Schoolcraft. Schoolcraft, whose research in Chippewa mythology had inspired Longfellow's "Song of Hiawatha," included a chapter on garden beds in his monumental six-volume collection of Indian lore published in 1851-57. He considered garden beds "by far the most striking and characteristic antiquarian monuments of this district of country."

Schoolcraft, Hubbard and most other early researchers were convinced that garden beds were truly agricultural in origin. Who built them was a knottier question. Their age, coupled with the fact that the various Algonquian tribes that had migrated into the Great Lakes region during the 17th century practiced only a primitive form of agriculture, eliminated them as the gardeners.

Schoolcraft and others concluded that the garden beds were probably constructed by elements of the "Mississippian" culture that had also built the extensive mounds found at Cahokia, Marietta and other Midwestern sites. By Schoolcraft's era several archaeologists had speculated that the mound builders had derived their culture from the Aztec civilization to the south. The garden beds, it would follow, were ruins of some type of sophisticated tillage system. Whether they enabled aboriginal farmers to grow corn and other crops on low-lying but fertile land subject to flooding, provided irrigation or, by their design, extended the growing season a few days remains an enigma.

Some 19th century historians pushed the concept of a prehistoric Midwestern civilization to the limit. Samuel Durant pondered in his "History of Kalamazoo," published in 1880, whether Kalamazoo's garden beds "could have been extensive plats where flowers were raised for the supply of some great city on Lake Michigan or in the Ohio Valley?"

The debate over who made the garden beds and why will probably never be resolved. Some archaeologists continue to advocate an agricultural use, others a ceremonial function. One reputable scholar suggested in 1957 that the beds were a hunting aid over which bison stumbled. Could they have been a signal to visitors from outer space?

Regardless of why they were built, the facts that they were and that the race that built them had been replaced by a more primitive culture by the time the white man arrived, highlight an historical axiom relevant to our planet's future. Schoolcraft summarized it in 1851: "The history of man, in his state of dispersion over the globe, is little more than a succession of advances and declensions, producing altered states of barbarism and civilization."

When George Washington Assassinated a Man From Niles

George Washington leads his men in an attack on Jumonville's reconnaissance party in 1754.

The Virginia militiamen stealthily surrounded the encamped French reconnaissance party on the morning of May 28, 1754. Despite the fact that Great Britain and France were at peace, Lt. Col. George Washington stepped forward into the clearing and gave the command to attack. The half-awake French soldiers rushed for their weapons, and the colonial marksmen poured a murderous hail of bullets into the camp.

It was all over in less than 15 minutes. Twenty-one unwounded Frenchmen surrendered and one escaped. Washington's Indian allies quickly brained and scalped the wounded. Ten French soldiers lay dead, including their commander, Joseph Villier le Sieur de Jumonville, who had grown up at Fort St. Joseph near present-day Niles.

The 22-year-old Washington had tasted his first military victory and thereby inadvertently precipitated a series of bloody wars between Great Britain and France that would rage until Napoleon's defeat at Waterloo in 1815. Washington found his first combat experience exhilarating and the sound of whistling musket balls quite "charming." But five weeks later, Louis Coulon de Villiers avenged his brother by defeating Washington at Fort Necessity. To his humiliation, Washington signed a document acknowledging that he had assassinated Jumonville although he later denied understanding the French term "l'assassinat."

Nicholas-Antoine Coulon de Villiers had arrived at Fort St. Joseph with his seven sons in 1724. From 1725 to 1730 he served as commandant at the only French post in western Michigan. Louis, who was 15 in 1725, and younger brother Joseph grew to manhood on what would become Michigan soil. Louis himself served as commandant at Fort St. Joseph from 1742-1745. The primary purpose of the post was to protect the French fur trade from encroachments by the British and their Indian allies.

During the 1740s, fur traders from Pennsylvania led by George Croghan and Conrad Weiser expanded their operations in the Ohio Valley. Also, a group of Virginia land speculators formed the Ohio Company and secured a large land grant on the upper Ohio that they planned to colonize with farmers from the coastal regions. The French, on the other hand, intended to hem in the British colonies through a string of forts established from Fort Niagara southward.

Lt. Governor Robert Dinwiddie of Virginia sent an ambitious 21-year-old surveyor named George Washington on a mission into the interior to protest the French expansion. Following a perilous journey, he returned in January 1754 to report that the French intended to occupy the entire Ohio Valley and could be repulsed only by military force.

To protect the interests of the Ohio Company, Dinwiddie ordered a fort built at the junction of the Allegheny and Monongahela Rivers (present-day Pittsburgh). A large French force, however, traveled from Montreal via Fort Niagara and Presque Isle (present-day Erie, Pa.) and thence by canoe to the forks of the Ohio. They surprised the work force of 40 Virginians engaged in building the fort, forced them to withdraw, destroyed the British fort and constructed Fort Duquesne nearby.

Washington learned of the French takeover while en route with an advance party of 150 soldiers sent to garrison the British post. Interpreting it as an act of war, he attacked Jumonville's party. Expecting retaliation, Washington withdrew to Great Meadows (now Uniontown, Pa.) and constructed a palisaded entrenchment he named Fort Necessity.

The French soldier who had escaped Washington's attack quickly carried the news to Fort Duquesne. When word of his brother's death reached Louis Villiers, then serving as commandant of Fort Chartres on the

Mississippi River near St. Louis, he set out with 300 Indians and 50 Frenchmen hot for revenge. At Fort Duquesne he was joined by 500 additional French troops.

Villiers reached Fort Necessity on the morning of July 3, 1754 and immediately attacked. Washington, unfortunately, had chosen a poor location for the fort, a river bottom surrounded by wooded hills. A furious rainstorm filled trenches with water, and much of Washington's powder supply got wet. French sharpshooters hiding behind trees began picking off the colonial troops as well as their horses, cattle and camp dogs.

Washington's men held out bravely, but by nightfall one-third of the force was dead or wounded. Rain-soaked and shivering, the remainder of the troops got into the rum supply brought along as a present for the Indians and soon were roaring drunk. Washington resisted the first French surrender demands, but after negotiating over the terms signed the capitulation about midnight. The Colonials were allowed to withdraw with their weapons and whatever supplies they could carry the next morning. The French promptly demolished the stockade.

Washington returned to the Fort Duquesne area the following year to experience a far worse defeat. He was part of Gen. Edward Braddock's army which was virtually wiped out at the Battle of the Wilderness.

Louis Villiers took over as commandant at Fort Niagara in 1756. He distinguished himself in the French victories at Forts Oswego and William Henry, but died of smallpox on November 2, 1757.

The initial French victories in what became known as the French and Indian War were reversed in 1759 with the fall of Quebec. The following year, Major Robert Rogers captured Detroit and Michilimackinac, and the British flag flew over Michigan for the next 36 years.

Rogers' Rangers
at Bloody Run

Major Robert Rogers, colorful ranger commander.

The sharp crackle of musket fire and the booming of cannon had brought the garrison at Fort Detroit to full alert during the early morning hours of July 29, 1763. The British soldiers peered over the palisades into the swirling fog that shrouded the Detroit River. Suddenly a bateau shot out of the mist, followed by another and another, each furiously paddled by red coats. The troops on the ramparts burst into cheers. The long-awaited relief force had miraculously ran the river gauntlet past the hordes of hostile Indians who had besieged the fort since May 9.

Following victory over the French in 1760, British commander Jeffery Amherst had tightened control over the lucrative Michigan fur trade. Stringent regulation required Indians to bring pelts directly to trading posts, lowered prices, and eliminated traditional good will gifts. Worse yet, the notoriously haughty British bearing toward native races stung Indian pride. In reaction, the western tribes took to the warpath in 1763 in what became known as Pontiac's Rebellion.

Pontiac, a crafty and charismatic Ottawa chief, centered his energies on reducing strategically important Fort Detroit. His original attempt at slaughtering the garrison by gaining entrance to the fort under the guise of a parley had failed when fort commander Major Henry Gladwin learned in advance of the ruse. But Pontiac's Ottawa, Potawatomi, and Chippewa followers butchered the British outside the fort and the siege was on.

Within weeks, Michilimackinac, St. Joseph and all other British posts west of Niagara fell to the Indians. The first unit Amherst sent to relieve Detroit was defeated and turned back 24 miles short of its goal. Amherst then placed his aid, Captain James Dalyell, in command of a larger relief force numbering 200 men that set out by boat from Niagara on July 7.

Major Robert Rogers, colorful ranger leader who had

won fame during the French and Indian War for his many daring forays against overwhelming odds, guided the relief expedition with 20 of his experienced rangers. Coasting along the southern shore of Lake Erie and pausing only to destroy a Wyandotte village near Sandusky, the force sneaked past the unsuspecting Indians near Detroit with little loss, thanks to the heavy fog.

Pontiac's main Indian army, some 2,000 strong, had recently withdrawn its camp to a marsh two miles upstream from Detroit. Dalyell, brave but inexperienced in Indian fighting, worried that the Indians might withdraw into the wilderness before he had a chance to soundly defeat them. He convinced Gladwin, against his better judgement, to allow him to conduct a sortie against the Indian camp.

At 2:30 on the moonlit morning of July 31, 247 soldiers including Rogers and a company of Queen's Rangers stealthily slipped out the fort's gate and marched two abreast up the road that ran east along the river. Two gunboats armed with small cannon protected Dalyell's right flank. But a resident of the French village surrounding the fort had warned Pontiac of the attack. A large force of Indians lay in ambush at a steep ravine through which gurgled Parent's Creek. Before the morning was over the stream would become known as Bloody Run.

As Dalyell's men tramped across the bridge over the creek, with hideous war whoops the Indians opened fire. A heap of dead and wounded soldiers littered the bridge. The troops returned fire but could aim at little except the flash of Indian muskets. Rogers who had lived through many another ambush immediately sought cover. He and his rangers stormed a nearby house. A group of panic-stricken regulars also made its sanctuary.

As the rangers piled packs of furs and furniture against the windows of the stout structure, some of the regulars discovered a keg of whiskey and began quaffing the fiery beverage. Meanwhile the master of the house, Jacques Campau, prevented the frightened soldiers from seeking shelter among the women who had taken refuge in the basement by standing on the trap door. Indian bullets spattered against the walls and whizzed inside through crevices.

When one of the gunboats temporarily drove the Indians off with raking cannon fire, Rogers and his men rushed out to join the main body of retreating troops. They scrambled out one door as some of the attacking Indians leaped through another. The British fled the mile and a half back to the fort while the Indians peppered them from behind cover. To fall wounded meant certain death by scalping knife. Dalyell was killed during a brave charge on a group of Indians holed up in a basement excavation.

Total British losses numbered 23 dead and 34 wounded. Pontiac had given the troops "a damm'd drubbing" as one veteran admitted. But it was not the total annihilation he had planned. Strengthened by the survivors of Bloody Run and reprovisioned by several vessels that landed at the fort, Gladwin held out. Pontiac's army gradually melted away. Following Col. Henry Bouquet's victory over eastern tribes at the Battle of Bushy Run near Pittsburg, Pontiac ended his siege and retreated to the Illinois Country. In 1769 a Peoria tribesman assassinated him.

Tough ranger Rogers experienced a checkered career. He traveled to London in 1765 to be lionized as a backwoods hero. There he published two books and one of the first plays penned by an American, "Ponteach." Through influential friends he had made in England, Rogers secured appointment as commandant at Fort Michilimackinac in 1766. There, against orders from superiors, he dispatched an expedition under Jonathan Carver to discover a northwest passage, helped negotiate a peace treaty between the warring Chippewa and Sioux and encouraged a more liberal fur trade policy.

Some subordinates proved treacherous, however, and Rogers was arrested for treason, shackled in painful irons during the long northern winter and finally transported to Montreal for trial, at which he was acquitted. Despite service in the Loyalist army during the Revolutionary War he never regained his former glory. The man who had established a tradition for tough soldiering that was emulated by ranger battalions in World War II died in obscurity in London in 1795.

The site of "Bloody Run," ca. 1885.

They Scared the Hell
Out of Hull

HULL IN FORT DETROIT.

General William Hull ponders the surrender of Detroit in 1812.

Fifteen-year-old Pvt. John Richardson swallowed hard, his eyes riveted on the two great cannons planted in the road ahead. Five weeks before, he had volunteered to give his life if necessary to repulse the numerically superior army that was invading his country. Now, on the morning of August 16, 1812, as part of a force of approximately 700 soldiers and 600 Indian allies that was attacking a strong fort garrisoned with some 2,000 troops, Richardson found himself marching straight into the face of death.

He could plainly see the enemy gunners with lighted fuses ready to touch off the cannons. His regiment marched on, straight up the road. The Detroit River on the right and a chain of houses on the left allowed no room for deployment. Minutes felt like hours as they marched forward, waiting, waiting for the puff of smoke and the muzzle blast, waiting to be mowed down by grapeshot.

Miraculously, the guns remained silent. Within three-fourths of a mile of the battery the terrain opened up and the column wheeled to the left through an orchard. The troops were covered, out of danger for the moment.

Shortly after, they saw it - a white flag, being carried down from the fort into their lines. There was a brief parley and then the unbelievable news spread quickly through the troops. American Gen. William Hull had surrendered Detroit to them - the British!

The United States and Great Britain had muddled into war in 1812, a war that neither nation really wanted to fight. The basic issues, impressment of American seamen into the British navy, maritime independence for America, and British intrigue in supplying and inciting Indians against the frontier, were being worked out diplomatically when President James Madison proclaimed a state of war with Great Britain on June 19th.

Despite the machinations of a group of Southern and Western congressmen known as war hawks and a lust for Canada by some, the country remained divided over prosecution of the war. Great Britain, drained by the Napoleonic Wars, certainly did not want another theater of operations. Yet war came, as a result of lack of communications, misunderstanding, ministerial vacillation and vocal minorities.

The initial U.S. plan of attack called for a three-pronged assault into Richardson's homeland of Canada: via Lake Champlain to Montreal, along the Niagara River frontier and from Detroit into southern Canada.

Before the war, Gen. Hull, a 58-year-old Revolutionary War hero who had served as governor of the Michigan Territory since its formation in 1805, had been placed in command of the Western army, 1,200 soldiers who had been recruited in Ohio.

On June 1, 1812, Hull's army set out for Detroit to deal with the threat posed by a gathering of Indians under Tecumseh. They moved slowly, struggling through the infamous wilderness south of Toledo known as "the black swamp."

On June 30 they finally reached the Maumee River, the present site of Toledo. Hull had yet to learn that war had been declared.

To make the remaining march to Detroit easier, he loaded entrenching tools, hospital supplies and other heavy equipment aboard the schooner, Cuyahoga. He also made the blunder of placing on the vessel a chest containing his military orders, muster rolls and official correspondence.

The British, who already knew of the declaration of war, captured the Cuyahoga as it sailed past Fort Malden on the Canadian shore. Hull learned of this devastating loss when he reached Frenchtown, present-day Monroe, on July 2. There he also first read that war had been declared two weeks before.

Three days later he reached Detroit, linking up with 600 Michigan militiamen who had been recruited to protect Detroit. Those added troops and others who had joined him brought his total command to more than 2,200 men with 43 cannons.

The fort at Detroit had recently been strengthened by 14-foot-high log palisades surrounded by an 8-foot-deep ditch lined with sharpened stakes. The British force at Fort Malden, across the Detroit River, numbered approximately 500 men.

Despite these overwhelming odds, Hull displayed little appetite for fighting, especially against Indians. War paint and breechcloths, tomahawks and scalping knives, ambush and torture - frankly, the Indians scared the hell out of Hull. By July 12, however, his subordinate officers, including Col. Lewis Cass, had goaded him into invading Canada.

Hull's 2,200 troops successfully crossed the river without loss and moved toward Fort Malden. But when a reconnaissance party reported a concentration of Indians ahead, Hull ordered his army to entrench.

While probing the area near Fort Malden, Cass' regiment encountered a force of Canadian militia at the Aux Canards River. In a brilliant maneuver Cass dislodged the Canadians and sent them running back to Fort Malden. His victory at this first battle of the War of 1812 won Cass the title "Hero of Tarontee," after the Indian name for the stream.

But Hull ordered Cass back, contending that he was too close to the enemy for safety. During the following two weeks Hull dallied, sending out small units of skirmishers only. His men grew more and more convinced of his ineptitude. Then on August 7, Hull suddenly ordered his army to retreat back across the river without even attacking the fort.

Two intelligence reports had unnerved him. Gen. Isaac Brock, lieutenant governor of Upper Canada, was reported en route with reinforcements. Worse yet, Fort Michilimackinac had surrendered on July 17. Hull later

40

defended his actions by writing "the surrender of Fort Mackinac opened the northern hive (of Indians) and they were swarming down in every direction."

Safely back in the fort at Detroit, Hull received another scare through a clever ruse. The British had deliberately allowed a letter to fall into his hands addressed to Capt. Roberts at Michilimackinac that referred to 5,000 Indians about to advance on Detroit. Hull became convinced that all of Michigan was about to be slaughtered. He ordered his men not to fire on the British invasion force that had assembled across the river in order not to pique the Indians.

Brock on the other hand, began a heavy artillery bombardment on Detroit on August 15. Against orders, some American batteries returned fire, but Hull ordered the rest of the troops to remain within the crowded fort. The evening of the 15th, Tecumseh and 600 braves crossed the river below Detroit and the following morning Brock's troops passed over unopposed.

Fearful that 800 civilians at Detroit would be slaughtered by the Indians should a battle begin, Hull capitulated without firing a shot. He also took the liberty of surrendering those troops not in the fort, including Cass and his regiment.

Upon hearing that, Cass, as the legend goes, broke his sword over his knee rather than surrender it to the British. That winter he traveled to Washington to press charges of cowardice, incompetence and treason against Hull. The following year he replaced Hull as governor of the Michigan Territory.

Hull was found guilty of cowardice and incompetence at his court martial in 1814 and sentenced to be shot. But President Madison pardoned him out of respect for his Revolutionary War record.

Hull spent the rest of his life trying to vindicate his name. The man who committed what was often termed "the most disgraceful deed in American history" died in 1825.

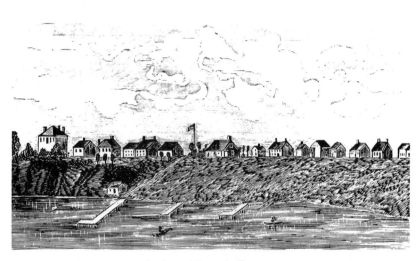

A view of Detroit in 1811.

In 1819, Chippewa Land
"Melted Like a Cake of Ice"

Louis Campau, who founded Saginaw and Grand Rapids.

Louis Campau, founder of Saginaw and Grand Rapids, leaped from the platform where the Treaty of Saginaw had been negotiated and struck Jacob Smith, Flint's first settler, "two heavy blows in the face." But before the kicking, eye-gouging and nose-biting essential to a good frontier affray could begin, a group of onlookers pulled the two fur traders apart. It was September 24, 1819, and if anyone deserved to be fighting mad it was the 114 Chippewa chiefs who had just signed away six million acres of ancestral land, a wedge-shape tract stretching from Kalamazoo to White Rock to Alpena, for a few trade goods, $3,000 cash and promise of a $1,000-a-year-payment.

The first major land cession by Michigan Indians, encompassing the southeastern portion of the territory, had taken place at the Treaty of Detroit in 1807. The United States had pledged the sum of $1,666.66 to the Chippewa by its terms. But the government had somehow failed to keep its promise, a delinquency that undoubtedly helped influence the Chippewa to back the British in the War of 1812. After the war, additional white settlers began encroaching onto the rich lands still under Indian control.

Consequently, Secretary of War John C. Calhoun directed Michigan Territorial Governor and Indian Agent Lewis Cass to negotiate an additional cession of Indian land. Calhoun also instructed Cass to get the Indians to agree to move west, beyond the Mississippi, thus once and for all eliminating this hinderance to Michigan's future development.

Cass had sent Louis Campau ahead to summon the Saginaw Valley Chippewa to a great council to be held at Saginaw and to prepare suitable quarters. Campau had operated a trading post situated at the present intersection of Hamilton and Clinton streets since 1815. He constructed a crude assembly hall nearby, some 200 feet long, made by interlacing branches over living tree trunks.

Prior to departing for Saginaw, Cass had borrowed from Detroit bankers the $1,666.66 owed from the last treaty so as to give these further negotiations a semblance of honesty. He sent ahead two ships loaded with an infantry company and supplies which made their way up the river to Saginaw. Cass, his staff and interpreters journeyed to Saginaw on horseback, arriving there on September 10, 1819.

Chippewas and a few Ottawas, variously estimated at from 1,500 to 4,000, had assembled at Saginaw. The first council that convened the morning of the 11th did not bode well for Cass's success. After Cass had stated his objective - and he wisely decided not to press for removal to the west at that time - Chief O-ge-maw-keke-too spoke:

"You do not know our wishes. Our people wonder what has brought you so far from your homes. Your young men have invited us to come and light the council fire. We are here to smoke the pipe of peace, but not to sell our lands. Our American father wants them. Our English father treats us better; he has never asked for them. Your people trespass upon our hunting grounds. You flock to our shores. Our waters grow warm; our land melts like a cake of ice; our possessions grow smaller and smaller; the warm wave of the white man rolls in upon us and melts us away. Our women reproach us. Our children want homes: shall we sell from under them the spot where they spread their blankets? We have not called you here. We smoke with you the pipe of peace."

Cass responded that "the Great White Father at Washington had just closed a war in which he had whipped the English King and the Indians too." The Indians' land belonged to the Americans by right of conquest, but out of the goodness of their hearts they would pay for it and allow ample tribal reservations where they could live unmolested, receive aid and be instructed in agriculture.

The council ended for that day as the chiefs sullenly

45

stalked back to their wigwams. For several days Cass and the other commissioners tried without success to break the impasse. In the meantime, however, Jacob Smith was busy conducting behind-the-scenes negotiations. Smith, who had long been a fur trader at various sites on the Flint and Saginaw Rivers, was well respected by the Chippewa. In particular, he was a good friend of the powerful chief Neome, whose village lay at the present site of Montrose.

Smith succeeded in convincing Neome to accept the treaty, provided there were reservations of several thousand acres for each of the various bands, including a 40,000-acre plat along the Flint River where his own village lay. Neome also insisted on a grant of approximately 7,000 acres at the present site of Flint to be awarded to 11 Indian children. A slip of paper containing their names was passed to the commissioners. The commissioners later discovered that five of them were Indian spellings of the names of Smith's own children living in Detroit.

The chiefs assembled on the afternoon of September 24 for the treaty signing and distribution of $3,000 in silver half dollars. Smith had one more trick up his sleeve. The chiefs had earlier agreed to pay $1,500 of that sum directly to Louis Campau in payment for goods he had advanced them. But Smith and two other traders planned on getting the cash themselves. Smith encouraged two drunken chiefs to demand full payment directly to them and as a result Campau got nothing. At that point he jumped from the platform and punched Smith twice.

The fight was broken up, but Campau got the rest of his revenge later that evening. In celebration of the treaty, Cass had provided five barrels of whiskey for the Indians - not enough, he figured, to get them too drunk. But Campau opened ten barrels of his own whiskey and passed it out liberally with a dipper. By 10:00 p.m., the

Indians were roaring drunk.

Cass ordered Campau to stop handing out liquor and stationed an armed guard around his store. A scuffle broke out and one of the soldiers bayoneted an Indian in the thigh. Suddenly Cass's quarters and the store were surrounded by whooping Indians brandishing tomahawks. Cass appeared in the door in his nightdress and called out, "Louis! Louis! Stop the liquor,Louis."

Campau replied, "General, you commenced it; you let Smith plunder me and rob me, but I will stand between you and all harm." The white men survived that night, but as Campau later remarked, "I lost my money; I lost my fight; I lost my liquor; but I got good satisfaction."

Seven years later, Campau purchased a tract of land that ultimately developed into the city of Grand Rapids. Smith built a trading post at the present site of Flint in 1819 where he lived until his death in 1825. The Saginaw Valley Chippewa retained title to their reservations until they too were lost during another treaty made in 1836.

Governor Lewis Cass, who got a scare in Saginaw.

Bishop Baraga: Apostle to the Chippewas

Bishop Frederic Baraga, "Apostle to the Chippewa."

From shore they were dark specks in a frozen wilderness of white, moving ever so slowly along the horizon. Closer, the specks became men, black-robed Father Frederic Baraga and his half-breed guide Basil Cadotte, shuffling along far out on the ice of Lake Superior.

It was spring 1836, and the travelers had left at dawn from Baraga's Indian mission at La Pointe on Wisconsin's Madeline Island. Their destination, the mouth of the Ontonagon River, lay 60 miles due east. To hug the ragged shore piled high with icy mountains would have lengthened their journey by days. Instead, they chose to cross the open ice, a hazardous but faster route.

Suddenly Cadotte saw blue water straight ahead. He turned and ran back, shouting for Baraga to follow. Then he skidded to a stop just short of the water's edge. They were adrift on a large cake of ice and the wind was blowing it out into Lake Superior! Cadotte cried, "We are lost mon Pere! We are lost!"

Baraga calmed him down, explaining that whatever happened, God's will would be done. Then they prayed and sang hymns in Chippewa while pacing the ice flow to keep warm from the sharp wind. Periodically, with a loud snap, pieces broke off their icy craft. At any minute it might crack beneath their feet and they would be in cold Lake Superior's waters where a man's life could be reckoned in minutes.

It was nearly nightfall when Cadotte shouted joyously, "Land, mon Pere!" Miraculously, the wind had shifted and they were being blown back toward the beach. The shore got closer and closer, beyond they could see the Porcupine Mountains. Slowly the cake of ice carried its passengers safely to Union Bay, near where they had originally intended to camp for the night. "You see," said Baraga, "we have traveled far and yet worked but little."

That adventure was but one of many that filled Baraga's 37-year career as "apostle to the Chippewas." Born June 29, 1797, in the Austrian Duchy of Carniola, now part of Yugoslavia, Baraga was heir to the castle of Malavas. He received an excellent education and became particularly adept at languages, including English, French, Italian and Spanish. Following graduation from the University of Vienna he studied in a Catholic seminary for two years and was ordained a priest in 1823. He renounced all worldly goods, deeding his large estate to his two sisters.

In 1830, Baraga joined the Leopoldine Society, which had been formed the previous year to promote missionary activity among the American Indians. He arrived in New York City on December 31, 1830 and traveled by stage to Cincinnati. That winter he studied the Ottawa language in preparation for his new post in northern Michigan. In the spring of 1831, Baraga began his journey north, performing missionary work en route. He found so many "lukewarm Catholics" in Ohio that he nearly decided to stay there. But his superior, Bishop Fenwick, convinced him that he could do more good among Michigan's Indians.

After a brief visit with another priest at Mackinac, he arrived at the major Ottawa settlement of L'Arbre Croche, the present site of Harbor Springs, on May 15. The Indians were delighted to learn that they would have a resident "Black Robe." "Happy day," Baraga wrote his sister on June 10, "that placed me among the Indians, with whom I will now remain uninterruptedly to the last breath of my life."

Baraga's labors were prodigious. He routinely rose at 3:00 a.m. for two hours of prayer and then plied his pastoral duties until 10:00 p.m. He traveled into the wilderness by snowshoe and canoe to establish itinerant missions at Beaver Island, Little Detroit Island, Manistique and Little Traverse. During the long northern winter when travel was nearly impossible, Baraga wrote and translated religious works into Ottawa.

In the summer of 1832, Baraga traveled to Detroit to supervise the printing of an Ottawa prayer book he had composed. While there, he delivered the funeral sermon for Father Richard, who had fallen victim to the cholera epidemic that ravaged the city. By the following summer Baraga had been so successful at L'Arbre Croche that he sought new fields of conquest.

He learned of the major Ottawa villages that lay along the Grand River, where reportedly there dwelt 900 Indians, practically all "genuine heathens." Baraga first visited the Indian village located on the west bank of the Grand River at the present site of Grand Rapids on June 15, 1833. He was warmly welcomed by Louis Campau, founder of the city. But Rev. Leonard Slater, who had been operating a Baptist mission there since 1827, vigorously campaigned against this competitor for Indian souls. Nevertheless, Baraga gained 86 converts during his three-week stay, a success rate that encouraged him to establish a permanent mission at Grand Rapids.

Following a tour of his northern missions, he returned to Grand Rapids in September. By April 1834 Baraga had erected a hewn-log chapel on the west side of the river between Watson and Butterworth streets, east of Lexington Avenue. Before the year was over, he also established an Indian school at Grand Rapids and a mission at the present site of Muskegon.

Despite these successes, he faced opposition not only from Slater and his Baptist converts but from the resident fur traders. Baraga, it seems, was interfering with their lucrative profession of swapping firewater for furs. One night his enemies instigated a drunken mob of Indians into attacking him. For hours they besieged his cabin as he knelt on the floor in prayer until an acting U.S. marshall dispersed them.

Baraga relinquished his Grand Rapids mission to Father Andreas Viszosky in February 1835. He served as pastor of the Marine City parish until June, when he returned to his beloved north country. This time he established a mission among the Chippewa, who spoke a language similar to the Ottawa, at La Pointe.

Over the next three decades Baraga devoted his life to the spiritual welfare of the Chippewa who lived along the southern shore of Lake Superior. He suffered privation and unbelievable hardship and experienced many narrow brushes with death as he routinely made long journeys to isolated villages. In 1843, he moved his headquarters to L'Anse, at the foot of Keweenaw Bay.

Ten years later, Baraga was consecrated the first bishop of the newly created Diocese of the Upper Peninsula. His first episcopal see at Sault Ste. Marie was relocated to Marquette in 1866. Despite the rigors of his Upper Peninsula career, Baraga found time to publish nine religious volumes in Chippewa between 1837 and 1850. His monumental Grammar of the *Ojibway Language* (Detroit: 1850) and *Chippewa Dictionary* (Cincinnati: 1853) remain classics in the field.

Baraga died in 1868. His remains were interred in a vault in the cathedral at Marquette. Baraga County, the city of Baraga and Baraga State Park honor his memory.

Sile Doty: Michigan's Greatest Thief

Sile Doty, horse thief, par excellence.

Sile Doty, "the most noted thief and daring burglar of his time," padded in his stocking feet along the upstairs corridor of the United States Hotel located on Woodbridge Street in Detroit. It was 1 o'clock on a spring morning in 1836.

Doty paused before the door of a room, listening intently. The only sound he heard was the drunken snoring of a state legislator. Doty examined a large ring of keys of every conceivable size and shape by the light of a "dark lantern," selected a likely looking one and stealthily unlocked the door. Tiptoeing inside, he quickly rifled the room until he discovered the official's stash of "shiners." Doty soon repeated that procedure on two other hotel guests, also state legislators, netting more than $500 in the process.

The hotel clerk, an accomplice who had led the lawmakers on a drunken binge to Detroit's red-light district earlier in the evening, then let the burglar out the hotel's back door. When the legislators opened their bleary eyes later that morning to find their money gone, they rushed to the clerk to discover how it could have happened. He told them they had probably lost their cash in one of the bordellos they had visited the night before. At that point, the legislators decided not to involve the authorities in the case.

Doty described that caper and scores of others in a lengthy autobiography posthumously published in 1880. He spent much of his 76-year career of crime in Michigan. Unrepentant to the end, the only thing he ever regretted was getting caught.

Born in St. Albans, Vermont in 1800, Doty, as his mother recalled, learned to steal before he could even walk. The light-fingered infant crept off with and hid anything within reach. His own earliest recollections were of secreting his siblings' playthings and watching them vainly search for them. At school, items ranging from classmates' hats to the teacher's penknife proved irresistible to the young scoundrel.

His family immigrated to Bangor, New York in 1809, where by the time he was 12 he had established a lucrative fur trade, stolen from the traps of others. As a teenager he learned to blacksmith and before long had manufactured a nice set of master keys and burglary tools. Doty specialized in stealing horses, unlocking barns in the night and making off with the finest teams in the area. He soon developed a good eye for champion horseflesh and chose the fastest mounts for his own getaways. When opportunity presented itself, however, he also enjoyed burglarizing stores and homes.

In 1834, Doty and wife, Sophia, surfaced in Adrian. He soon sniffed out a coterie of fellow thieves, counterfeiters, burglars, highwaymen and other "black legs" who resided between Toledo and Chicago. He organized a well-disciplined ring who assisted each other in getaways and fencing stolen goods. His coup over the drunken legislators in Detroit so impressed him with that city's possibilities that he moved there for two years. In 1837, he conducted a horse-stealing foray into Kentucky, returning not only with a nice string of equine booty but a young slave he had liberated as well.

A few years later, Doty committed his first murder, a companion who threatened to "squeal" on him. The body was accidentally discovered, with Doty arrested and brought to trial and sentenced to life imprisonment. But he busted out of jail and fled to Mexico on the sheriff's horse. There he linked up with General Zachary Taylor's invading army. By day he worked as a cook and each night diligently robbed and killed Mexican citizens.

Although he never officially enlisted, Doty found upon his return to Michigan that he had been pardoned as a result of his military service. He relocated his family to southwestern Branch County, where he pretended to farm. But robbery, and in particular horse-thieving, re-mained his real profession. He also routinely traveled to nearby towns in the dead of night to replenish anything his wife lacked in the way of provisions.

He gained a reputation as a Robin Hood, stealing from the rich to benefit the poor. Neighbors needing a new ox yoke or a supply of flour need only mention it and Doty soon provided them with someone else's property. When he noticed that a poor family slept on the floor, he promptly stole a bed from a Hillsdale furniture store and some bedding from a nearby hotel and delivered it to them.

Doty occasionally got caught and served several short stints in the Jackson State Penitentiary. In 1851, however, a Lenawee County judge grew weary of his recidivism. Thinking Doty 53 years old, the judge sentenced him to 17 years, a term he thought sufficient to last the Scriptural limit of three score and ten. But Doty fooled him. He served 15 years, and despite the fact that he continued his stealing within the prison walls and even fashioned a key that enabled him to visit the female department on occasion, he was released two years early for good behavior.

Less than one year after his release, however, Doty was convicted of horse stealing near Coldwater. He not only served that four-year term in Jackson, but another two-year burglary rap meted out in Cheboygan. The year before he died, Doty took on a young apprentice and the two shipped stolen property to Grand Rapids.

Doty died of "congestion of the liver" in 1876. His funeral held in Reading, Hillsdale County, was remembered by an acquaintance as "the most largely attended of any ever held there." He failed to mention whether the crowd consisted of mourners or citizens merely wanting to verify whether "Michigan's greatest thief" was truly dead.

Singapore, the Buried City

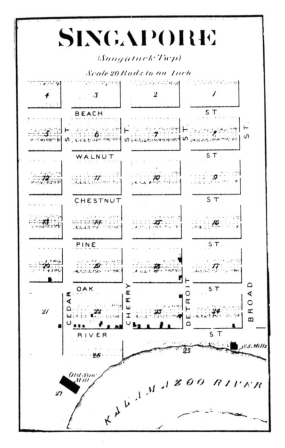

Plat of Singapore in 1873.

Like a great, tawny beast - beautiful but deadly - the towering sand dunes coil about the mouth of the Kalamazoo River. When the air is still the dunes silently sun themselves, but when the wind blows the singing sands stir, hungry to taste new surroundings. Little fingers of sand delicately probe all in their reach and the fingers grow to hands and the hands grow to strong sandy arms that pinion and smother whatever they hug. Beneath those restless dunes, on the north bank near where the river meets the great lake, lie the ruins of the forgotten city of Singapore, "Michigan's Pompeii."

Singapore, named after the Malaysian trading port - but why no one now knows for sure - was the brainchild of Oshea Wilder. Born in Gardner, Massachusetts in 1784, Wilder learned blacksmithing and surveying from his father. He served in the War of 1812, toured Europe during the early 1820s and then settled down in Rochester, New York.

When the opening of the Erie Canal in 1825 facilitated travel to Michigan Territory, western New Yorkers rushed for the peninsula's lush lands. Wilder succumbed to the Michigan fever in 1831, pioneering near Marshall in Calhoun County. There he built a sawmill and held a number of local political offices. Territorial Governor Stevens T. Mason appointed Wilder to a three-man commission charged with determining Allegan County's seat in 1834. While there, he recognized the value of the immense stands of white pine that grew along the Kalamazoo River north of Allegan.

In 1836, Wilder convinced four other New Yorkers to subscribe $25,000 to be invested in pine lands. He soon secured choice tracts on the lower Kalamazoo. By July 1836 Wilder had also conceived a notion that the mouth of the Kalamazoo was destined to become the site of a major metropolis. "There is but two or three points on Lake Michigan of more importance than this for a town," Wilder wrote his partners, "...except Grand River

(Grand Haven) it has the best natural harbor on the east side of the lake."

At first, Wilder wanted a tract at the mouth of the river owned by Horace Comstock, a speculator who founded the Kalamazoo County village that bears his name. But Comstock held his land too dearly and Wilder and associates settled for a cheaper site one mile upstream on the north side of a big "ox bow" bend in the river. By December 1836 Wilder had made arrangements to purchase a half-interest in a 100-acre parcel owned by the Boston Company, a syndicate that also founded the village of Allegan.

He sent a sketch map of the holdings to his partners. Ominously he labeled that portion north of the site "sand hills." Wilder soon had the land surveyed and the town of Singapore platted into lots. Cedar, Cherry, Detroit and Broad streets ran north from the river intersecting River, Oak, Pine, Chestnut, Walnut and Beach streets.

Wilder moved to Singapore the next spring to supervise construction of dwellings and a steam-powered sawmill. "It is the opinion of all well informed men that Singapore will not be second to any place on the east side of the lakeshore," he confidently reported to his partners.

To insure the city's success, Wilder sought to establish a bank there. Michigan's lax banking laws allowed practically anyone to create such an institution and issue paper currency provided they had one-third of its value in hard money. However, by the end of 1837 Wilder's New York partners had lost interest in Singapore, largely because of the depression that gripped the eastern states. They sold out to the Boston Company.

But the effects of the Panic of 1837 had not yet reached Michigan, where optimism remained strong. Wilder went ahead with his plans and chartered the Bank of Singapore on January 8, 1838. A New York firm printed $50,000 of ornate Singapore bills in various denominations. Wilder also imported bricks from out East with which he constructed a secure bank vault. In common with other so-called "Wild Cat Banks," however, the Singapore institution never actually had much real money in its vault. Its isolated location helped discourage redemption in hard money, and when Wilder got wind of the approach of a state bank examiner, legend has it, he temporarily borrowed specie from an Allegan bank. As the story goes, the canoe carrying the gold hit a snag in the Kalamazoo and the money bags sank to the bottom of the river. The bank examiner was wined and dined en route until a Singapore blacksmith could fashion a grapple hook that was used to fish out the assets. Nevertheless, Singapore notes soon depreciated - one settler remembered paying $40 face value for a darning needle - and the bank went belly up within the year.

In the meantime, a general store and a three-story hotel were opened in Singapore. By late Spring 1839, the steam-powered sawmill cut over 300,000 feet of lumber in about one month's time. But by then, the depression had reached the West and no one had cash to pay for lumber. The sawmill operation limped along for a year or so and then it too went bankrupt. The Singapore dream was over for Wilder. He moved back to Calhoun County where he died in 1846.

The residents who remained in Singapore barely survived the particularly harsh winter of 1842. Luckily for them, but not for the seven sailors who drowned, the steamer Milwaukee was wrecked about two miles up the coast. Some of its cargo, barrels of flour and wine, washed ashore to save Singapore from starvation.

By 1844 the worst of the depression was over. James G. Carter, a Massachusetts banker who had invested in Singapore, now owned it outright. He moved there to manage his property. Two years later the sawmill burned, and he sold out to his brother, Artemas, and

Francis B. Stockbridge. They rebuilt the mill and also launched at Singapore one of the first three-masted schooners on Lake Michigan, the Octavia, to carry their lumber to Chicago markets. Singapore prospered and Stockbridge became a wealthy man. He ultimately moved to Kalamazoo and served as a U.S. senator in 1887-1894.

Singapore's brief golden age began following the Civil War. In 1870 alone, 672 vessels cleared the mouth of the Kalamazoo carrying 30 million feet of lumber, 31 million shingles and other wooden products. The Singapore mill was the largest in the area. Following the Chicago fire of 1871, lumber to rebuild that city grew in great demand and lumberjacks rapidly cut the remaining pine along the lower Kalamazoo and its tributaries.

In 1873, Singapore's population numbered between 100 and 200, predominantly millworkers and their families, and 22 structures dotted its streets. But two years later, with the Kalamazoo River timber gone, Stockbridge and partners loaded the Singapore mill on a vessel and re-established it in St. Ignace. The neighboring Saugatuck newspaper lamented "nothing remains of a once thriving village but a few scattered houses." Some of Singapore's structures were salvaged and relocated elsewhere, but the hotel was too large to move. Jim Nichols, a fisherman, took squatter's rights to the ground floor of the hotel.

Relentlessly the sand dunes crept closer. Within a few years they had flowed into the hotel. Nichols moved to the second floor and the dunes followed. He retreated to the third floor and still the sand mounted. Finally all that could be seen of Singapore was the roof tip of the hotel. In 1894, two boys warmed themselves after a long winter's trek by setting fire to the rooftop. Today, whatever remains, if anything, of Singapore lies shrouded beneath a deep blanket of sand.

Caroline Kirkland, Literary Lady on the Frontier

Caroline Kirkland, Eastern literati on the Michigan frontier.

An occasional blaze scarring the gray skin of a big beech tree, here and there a jagged stump, a few poles laid across the worst of the mud holes, and a path of hoof-churned soil in the center marked the road from the interminable wilderness through which it snaked. Nevertheless, in Michigan of 1837 it was a highway.

A single set of fresh wagon tracks outlined the road's many convolutions. The deep imprint of the wheels disappeared into a particularly nasty swamp located a few miles east of the Livingston County settlement known as Pinckney. In the center of the swamp, surrounded by an expanse of inky black mud, stood a startling spectacle.

A heavy lumber wagon heaped high with fancy chairs, tables, trunks, potted plants, a cage of live chickens and other frontier incongruities had sunk up to its axles in the muck. A sleek greyhound lay curled on the rear of the vehicle, four towheaded children clambered over its sides, and ensconced in a comfortable armchair near the summit of the load sat a woman calmly reading a book of essays. The silk umbrella she tilted against the mid-summer's rays and her stylish apparel, including delicate paper-soled shoes, were in perfect fashion for a Broadway promenade.

Caroline Kirkland, one of the most sophisticated American women of her time, had arrived on the Michigan frontier.

Born Caroline Matilda Stansbury in New York City on January 11, 1801, she was the eldest child of a bookseller and publisher. She early developed a flair for languages, becoming adept in Latin, French, Italian and German. She spent her childhood reading the many books in her father's shop and her love of learning prompted her to gain an education uncommon for women of her time. Training in the social graces was not neglected; she also became well versed in music and dancing. As a teenager she began teaching in her aunt's school in New York City.

Following her father's death, she and her mother moved west in 1822 to Clinton, New York, the site of Hamilton College. There she met William Kirkland, a myopic and nearly deaf professor of classical literature. Six years later they were wed, and shortly thereafter the Kirklands founded a girls' school in Geneva, New York.

The 1830s witnessed a mass migration of western New Yorkers into Michigan Territory. The Kirklands caught the Michigan fever in 1835 and traveled to Detroit via the Erie Canal and a lake steamer. Kirkland became principal of the recently established Detroit Female Academy and his wife joined the teaching staff.

Detroit in 1835 was the staging area for an army of land speculators eager to carve fortunes out of choice tracts available at the government price of $1.25 per acre. It did not take Kirkland long to succumb to the land mania and by 1836 the pedagogue had become a town proprietor. He acquired control of 1,300 acres of timber and swamp land in southern Livingston County, and there founded a town named Pinckney in his brother's honor.

In the summer of 1837, Kirkland and his sophisticated wife, their four children and a greyhound named D'Orsay climbed aboard a wagon loaded down with fashionable furnishings ill-suited to frontier life and started out for their new home in the wilderness. Several long days of traveling later, the team that pulled the cumbersome vehicle had become so mired in the swamp previously alluded to that Kirkland had cut the traces. One of the frightened horses ran off and Kirkland had gone for help mounted on the other.

The experience of being marooned in the middle of a swamp had become, as Caroline later wrote, "a leetle tedious" by the time her husband returned three hours later to extricate the wagon. By dusk, the weary family had reached the primitive log cabin where they would live until a larger frame house could be erected.

Caroline found life on the frontier far worse than she had anticipated. The little one-room cabin afforded her no privacy. Use of the fireplace, the only place to cook, made the interior insufferably hot. The floor had cracks large enough to admit the rattlesnakes that sometimes crawled beneath it. Unused to performing her own domestic tasks, she had planned on hiring a maid to help her. But fellow settlers, despite their poverty, counted their freedom too dear to accept such a subservient position.

Caroline soon encountered other frontier peculiarities. Visitors, for example, routinely walked in without knocking and made themselves "right at home." One neighbor often showed up for tea, which she insisted on drinking directly from the spout of the teapot because "it tasted so better." At mealtime she grabbed the entire ham and cut off mouthfuls with her knife, declining aid from the carver with "I'll help myself, I thank ye, I never want no waitin' on."

The frontier custom of borrowing also proved vexing. A ragged neighbor girl appeared at her door to announce, "Mother wants your sifter, and she says she guesses you can let her have some sugar and tea, 'cause you've got plenty." To not share with the entire community was "an unpardonable crime." Consequently, Caroline found herself lending her broom, thread, spoons, thimble, scissors, shawl, shoes and cat. But when she drew the line at relinquishing her comb and her husband would not part with his best pair of pants, the Kirklands gained a reputation as "thinking they were better than others."

Caroline described her many humorous experiences on the Michigan frontier in a book titled, *A New Home-Who'll Follow!* Published in New York in 1839 under the nom de plume Mary Clavers, the volume drew enthusiastic praise from the Eastern literati and quickly went through three editions. Three years later she penned a sequel, *Forest Life.*

Despite her precaution in using a pseudonym, copies of her books found their way to Pinckney, where residents readily recognized the authoress as well as themselves among the thinly veiled characterizations.

Ostracized and nearly bankrupt, the Kirklands retreated back to New York in 1843. Caroline launched a career as a professional writer and magazine editor. Her home became a rendezvous for some of America's most gifted writers. Edgar Allen Poe, William Cullen Bryant and others praised her work.

Nearly blind and deaf, William Kirkland accidentally walked off a wharf in New York and drowned in 1846. Caroline Kirkland, who immortalized her unhappy frontier experiences in a Michigan classic, died of apoplexy in 1864.

Caroline Kirkland's A New Home... carried this engraving of a typical backwoods Michigan log cabin.

Whatever Happened to Little Willie Filley?

Jackson County pioneers search for the lost boy in 1837, but find only deer and bear.

Lydia Mount had warned little William Filley not to go near the swamp that lay between her log cabin and that of Filley's family located six miles south of the frontier settlement of Jackson. Not only was it infested with rattlesnakes, but plenty of black bears still prowled its thickets. What's more, few Jackson County pioneers had not heard the spine-chilling howl of wolves at night. The winter before, in fact, a wolf pack had killed and eaten an Indian in the northern part of the county. Settlers had found what was left of him and the bodies of seven wolves he had slain with his hatchet before they dragged him down.

Nevertheless, the 5-year-old boy had pleaded so incessantly to go along with Mrs. Mount's teen-aged daughter, Mary, into the swamp to pick whortleberries that she relented. It was about noon on August 3, 1837, when they left the cabin. Soon the little tyke grew tired. Mary led him by the hand to the beaten path that wound back to her cabin and left him to walk back. Several hours later she returned with a full bucket of berries and asked her mother where William was. He had not returned.

The Mount and Filley families began a desperate search for William, retracing Mary's path and hollering his name to no avail. Word soon spread throughout the Jackson area that the Filley boy was lost in the swamp and in true frontier fashion hundreds of pioneers joined the hunt. That night they lit enormous bonfires near the swamp.

About 10 p.m. members of the Hamilton family, who lived two miles to the west, thought they heard the stifled cry of a child. The next morning they found a letter nearby that had been given to William by his aunt. Some 800 people formed a huge circle around that location and began moving in, searching every square foot of swamp and forest for some sign of the boy. As the circle got smaller, three bears and some deer bolted through, but nothing else was found.

For weeks they continued the search, dragging nearby lakes and streams and thoroughly scouring the wilderness for a radius of 20 miles. Some grew suspicious of the Mount family and examined their buildings and ash heaps for the body of the child. All efforts proved futile.

Finally even the most stubborn gave up in despair of ever finding the child - all, that is, but Ammi Filley, who continued to roam the woods in search of his first-born son. Heartbroken, William's mother "went down in sorrow to an untimely grave," but still his father's voice was heard "late at night and early in the morning calling, William, William!"

Eight years passed and still the mystery haunted the Jackson community. Then Filley learned of a white child that had been taken from a roving band of Indians in New York and placed in an orphanage. The boy remembered living for a while in Michigan. Could he be the "long lost Jackson boy?" Alas, the results of a detailed investigation proved beyond doubt that this white captive was actually Paul Pry, a somewhat younger boy who had once resided near Hillsdale.

The years turned to decades. The Michigan Central Railroad snaked its way across the state, linking Jackson with Detroit and Chicago, settlers transformed the Jackson County wilderness into rich farmlands and brother fought brother for four years of bloody Civil War. But Ammi Filley languished, a ruined man, partially deranged at times.

Then, in October 1866, the Jackson postmaster received a cryptic letter sent from Coldwater: "Sir: -Not knowing your name, but thinking that you would do me the favor to try and ascertain whether there is a man living in the city of Jackson, where you live, or anywhere else, by the name of Willey. I am his son. I was taken by the Indians about thirty years ago. Can you find any of the relatives of this Willey? All that I know about it is that my father's name is Willey, and that I was taken from Michigan. This I was told by an Indian. Please to try and find out for me, and I will thank you, whether you find my father or not, as soon as you can make it convenient, as I want to see him or my relations. Your humble servant, William Willey." Could this be the "long lost Jackson boy?"

On October 19 a strange looking man, garbed in a crudely fashioned woolen suit and resembling more a Mormon elder than an Indian captive, arrived in Jackson. Friends and relatives thought they recognized in him the visage of the 5-year-old boy they had not seen in 29 years. So too did Ammi Filley who, summoned from his new residence in Illinois, clasped his son to his bosom in paternal affection.

William Filley, Jackson residents soon learned, had risen to the exalted rank of "Chief Medicine Man, Comanche Tribe, Rocky Mountains, Oregon." A skilled compounder of Indian herbal remedies, he also understood the secret of making steel out of iron with the aid of a liquid. He had lived among 17 different western tribes, spoke 11 Indian dialects and could carry a tolerable tune in English, Spanish and Indian.

J.Z. Ballard of Jackson, who had married one of William's sisters, rushed into print a book recounting the amazing adventures of the long lost Jackson boy. Stolen from the swamp by a passing band of Pottawatomi to avenge white encroachments on their ancestral land, young Filley went along when most of the tribe were herded west under the provisions of the Indian Removal Act.

The Potawatomi treated him well enough but for some reason they swapped him to another tribe. That tribe traded him to the Sioux, who in turn passed him along to the Crows and the Walla Wallas. Sensing that he might be of value to them as an intermediary in their dealings with the whites, the Indians enrolled Filley in a San

Francisco school where he relearned English.

From there, as he related to Ballard, Filley experienced a series of thrilling and well-nigh unbelievable adventures in the Rocky Mountains, routinely fighting grizzly bears, mountain lions and other savage beasts by hand. When a dying Indian chief told him of his true identity, Filley decided to return to Michigan to find his kin.

Unfortunately, not much else is known about the subsequent life of the long lost Jackson boy. Possibly he returned to the western tribes or, more probably, took to the road as a traveling medicine man.

One final tidbit does appear, however, in Col. Charles V. DeLand's *History of Jackson County*, published in 1903. DeLand, a pioneer resident of Jackson County who led a long distinguished life as a newspaper publisher, Civil War veteran and one of the founders of the Republican Party in 1854, wrote "Many people, including the writer, flocked to see him (Filley), but nobody was fully convinced of his identity."

Could this be the long lost Jackson boy?

Whitefish, "Food of the Nymphs"

Chippewa fishing in the St. Marys rapids, ca. 1900.

"I have eaten tunny in the gulf of Genoa, anchovies fresh out of the bay of Naples and trout of the Salzkammergut and diverse other fishy dainties rich and rare, but the refined whitefish exceeds them all," wrote Anna Jameson, a cultured British authoress who toured the north country in 1837. During a sojourn at Sault Ste. Marie, Mrs. Jameson dined on freshly caught whitefish four times a day and still pronounced them "the most luxurious delicacy that swims the waters." For centuries other literary travelers had similarly raved of Michigan's piscine treasures.

French explorers Pierre Esprit, Sieur de Radisson, and Medart Chouart, Sieur de Grosseilliers, tarried also at the Sault during an expedition to the Lake Superior country in 1659. There they "found the truth," wrote Radisson, "of what those men (the native Chippewa) often said, that if once we could come to that place we would make good cheer of a fish they call assickmack, which signifies a whitefish." The whitefish that abounded in the St. Marys rapids, in fact, formed a staple diet for the native "Salteurs" who dwelt there.

A decade after Radisson and Grosseilliers' expedition, Father Claude Dablon arrived at the Sault to take charge of the Jesuit mission that had been established by Father Marquette. Dablon penned a graphic description of the Indian mode of catching whitefish in the roaring rapids:

"Dexterity and strength are needed for this kind of fishing, for one must stand upright in a bark canoe and then, among the whirlpools, with muscles tense thrust deep into the water a rod at the end of which is fastened a net made in the form of a pocket, into which the fish are made to enter. One must look for them as they glide between the rocks, pursue them when they are seen and when they have been made to enter the net raise them suddenly by a strong pull into the canoe. This is repeated over and over, six or seven large fish being taken each time until the canoe is loaded. Not everyone is fitted for this kind of fishing, and it sometimes happens that persons lacking the requisite skill and experience over-turn the canoe."

Indeed, none but the resident Salteurs who knew every rock and eddy of the rapids had the skill to catch whitefish in the great "Sault" of the St. Marys. They continued to ply their ancient art as the British replaced the French and were in turn succeeded by Americans. Few travelers who visited the region failed to describe the picturesque birch-bark canoes bobbing in the fierce rapids.

The largest and most succulent whitefish, weighing from four to 14 pounds, came from the cold waters of Lake Superior and the Straits of Mackinac region. Whitefish caught in the Detroit River averaged about two pounds. Many of the French habitants at Detroit specialized in catching whitefish with a seine. Rowing into the stream, they dropped a net held up with floats, and pulled it to shore laden with silvery fish.

The Indians, French and British had been satisfied to consume whitefish to their heart's content. But enter-prising Yankees saw their fortunes in the finny delicacies. As the northern fur trade waned in the 1820s and '30s, commercial exploitation of whitefish began.

Surveyor Lucius Lyon, who would become one of Michigan's first U.S. senators in 1837, emigrated from Vermont to Detroit in 1821. In November 1822, he wrote a letter back home describing the territory's fishing in-dustry. One seine alone, Lyon had been informed, had already taken 1,600, 200-pound barrels of fish in Lake Superior. The shores of the Detroit River were "lined with fishermen and their nets." "One fishery night be-fore last," he wrote, "took 16,000 whitefish." They sold for a penny apiece at that time.

Captain Frederick Marryat, a British author who toured the Great Lakes in 1837, wrote that "at Mackinac alone they cure about 2,000 barrels (of whitefish and trout), which sell for $10 the barrel; at the Sault, about the same quantities,; and on Lake Superior at the station of the American Fur Company, they have commenced the fishing to lessen the expense of the establishment and they now salt down about 4,000 barrels; but this traffic is still in its infancy and will become more profitable as the west becomes more populous."

Marryat's prophecy proved true as more and more fishermen succumbed to the lure of the north country and its seemingly inexhaustible supply of whitefish. Commercial fishing techniques also became more efficient when, according to William H.G. Kingston, another British author who visited the Sault in 1853, a Brazilian fisherman introduced deep-sea type gill nets to the Great Lakes. They soon superseded the seine nets.

In 1853, also, James Jesse Strang, King of Beaver Island, described that area's commercial fishing industry in a letter to the Smithsonian Institute: "The whitefish are the most abundant and, as an article of commerce, the most valuable fish of this region. Fifty-thousand barrels per annum are taken among the Beaver Islands, and the quantity taken is rapidly increasing." Strang failed to mention in his article that his Mormon followers had crowded out the Irish fishermen who had formerly made a lucrative living off the island's rich fishing banks. Three years later, the animosity thus engendered would be one of the factors that cost Strang his life via assassination and the Irish once again dominated Beaver Island fishing.

Yankee ingenuity would also soon replace gill nets with an even more efficient mode of capturing whitefish - a method so successful that they were driven to near extinction within a few years. In 1858, according to S.H. Smith, a Charlevoix-based fisherman, "someone, somewhere, invented the pound net, which, in my opinion, proved to be the biggest curse to the fishing industry of anything in the whole fishing business ever."

Fish entered huge pound nets through a narrow funnel and were then trapped within. "A single pound net," wrote Smith, "could gather in more fish that were ready to spawn in a given time, than a hundred gill nets could have done." It was not necessarily the number taken that nearly spelled doom for the whitefish industry but the "barrels and barrels of spawn carried away with the offal and buried." No one bothered to save the ripe spawn for transplanting and within a decade "a pound net could not catch enough fish to pay the expense of operation."

The alarming decline of whitefish spurred the state to create the Michigan Fish Commission in 1873. Within a few years the Commission had begun artificially propagating millions of whitefish eggs at state fish hatcheries at Paris, Detroit and elsewhere and releasing the fry into the Great Lakes. By the turn of the century, however, the Commission had suspended efforts at restocking whitefish in favor of game fish. The whitefish population made a slow recovery, but it has never reached its earlier levels.

Today, through the efforts of small numbers of commercial fisherman, Michigan diners continue to enjoy the fish whose Latin name translates "food of the nymphs." Fresh or smoked, the only objection to the flesh of the whitefish is, as Dr. Daniel Drake observed in 1842, "he who tastes it once will thenceforth be unable to relish that of any other fish.

The Sweet, Beet-Bonanza

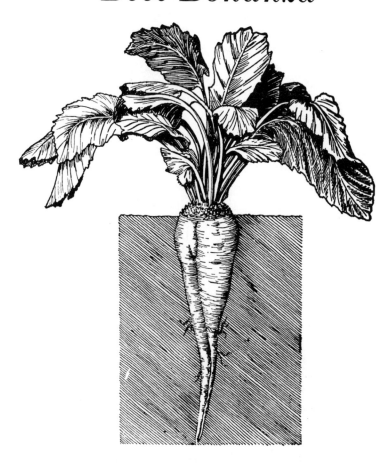

A healthy sugar beet.

One crisp October morning in 1838, Chapman Yates, co-proprietor of Michigan's first sugar beet factory, stood outside his plant in White Pigeon watching a farmer unload a wagon heaped with the big ugly vegetables. The beets bobbed up and down in a water chute en route to the washing line.

Shivering a little, Yates walked to the plant and entered its steamy interior. He heard the slushy grating noise made as a laborer holding a wooden block pushed beets against a big revolving rasp. Another workman busily shoveled the pulp into gunny sacks and piled them under a screw press. When several layers of sacks had been arranged under the press, it slowly creaked down. The beet sap squirted out onto a trough and was conveyed by a leather hose to a cistern in the boiling room. Other workers mixed in a dash of slaked lime and evaporated the sap into rich syrup.

Yates furrowed his brow at the thought of the gallons and gallons of molasses he had thus produced. For try as he might, the technology for rendering the molasses into sugar crystals had eluded him. Unless he managed to produce sugar he would lose out on the two cents per pound bounty the State Legislature had generously offered.

The science of converting beets to sugar had been discovered by a German chemist named Marggraf in 1747. Nothing much had come of his alchemy, however, until the early 19th century when Napoleon had promoted the manufacture of beet sugar in an attempt to hamstring Great Britain's lucrative colonial commerce in cane sugar. The first factory established on the continent in 1809 proved so successful that cultivation of sugar beets became a major enterprise in France and Germany.

The pioneer American sugar beet plant, established in Philadelphia in 1830, was followed by the White Pigeon experiment. In 1839, the Michigan Legislature further sweetened the pot by passing a bill authorizing a $5,000 loan to the White Pigeon Beet Sugar Co. The following year, Lucius Lyon reported that the White Pigeon proprietors had commissioned future governor John S. Barry of Constantine to travel to France to hire artisans skilled in sugar making.

In the meantime, Lyon, a government surveyor, land speculator and entrepreneur extrordinaire, had been dabbling in sugar beets himself. During the spring of 1839 he made a trip to Rochester, N.Y., where he acquired some French sugar beet seeds. Lyon planted 30 acres of beets at his farm near the Ionia County village he had founded and named after himself. He harvested 10 tons to the acre that fall but never succeeded in converting any beets to sugar. Neither, apparently, did the White Pigeon operation. It went bankrupt in 1840.

Nearly 60 years would pass before Michiganians again ventured into the sugar beet business. In the interim there had been a few voices crying in the wilderness. The Michigan Agricultural Society, for example, had published a paper in its 1869 annual report concerning the profitable sugar beet industry in Europe. In 1884, Joseph Seeman, pioneer Saginaw journalist and co-founder of the Saginaw News, visited Bohemia, the country of his birth. There he became intrigued with beet sugar. He began promoting the cultivation of sugar beets in his German-language newspaper, the Saginaw Zeitung, and the Saginaw Evening News.

Seeman also imported sugar beet seeds which he gave to Professor Robert C. Kedzie of the Michigan Agricultural College in East Lansing. Kedzie conducted experiments in the Saginaw Valley in 1891 and found the soil excellent for cultivation of sugar beets.

In 1897, 600 Saginaw County farmers participated in a sugar beet project financed by local lumbermen seeking to find a way to utilize their vast holdings of cut-over land. An exhibition of the prize sugar beets they had grown held that fall in a vacant store on Genesee

Avenue "opened the eyes of the community" to the potential of the novel crop.

The year 1897 brought two other developments of even greater significance. Congress passed the protectionist Dingley tariff which levied an overall tax of 57 percent on many imported goods, including cane sugar. Also, the state Legislature voted another bounty on Michigan-made sugar - 1 cent per pound this time.

Alert Bay City businessmen beat Saginaw to the punch by erecting the valley's first sugar beet factory in Essexville. The Michigan Sugar Co. plant began slicing its first beets on October 14, 1898.

The primitive rasping and squeezing technology had been replaced by the more efficient diffusion process of extracting sap from sliced beets. The initial success of the Essexville plant spurred a statewide rush for the beet bonanza. By the fall of 1899 additional sugar factories had opened in Bay City, Rochester, Caro, Benton Harbor, Holland, Alma and Kalamazoo.

By 1901 West Bay City, Lansing, Marine City and Saginaw also sported sugar plants. Five years later, the completion of a factory in Charlevoix brought the state's total to 23, including one in the U.P. at Menominee. Together they produced more than 173 million pounds of sugar in 1906.

But a number of factors were already bringing a reversal to the sugar beet boom: The state had dropped its penny-a-pound bonus in 1900. Transportation costs to some factories located too far from the prime sugar beet growing areas ate into profits. Cutthroat competition by Eastern "sugar magnates" sought to smother Michigan's infant industry in the cradle.

By 1909 six Michigan factories had closed and many others soon followed. This came as a mixed blessing for some communities, however. A young papermaker named Jacob Kindleberger, for example, moved his operation into the abandoned sugar beet factory near Kalamazoo. His Kalamazoo Vegetable Parchment Co. soon put Parchment, the company town that developed around it, on the map.

In 1906 six faltering companies with plants at Alma, Bay City, Caro, Carrollton, Croswell and Sebewaing merged to form the dominant Michigan Sugar Co. It consolidated operations in the region that became known as the "Sugar Bowl of the Midwest."

Saginaw Valley and thumb area growers still enjoy a sweet success story.

A 1906 bird's-eye view of the Michigan Sugar Co. Plant located in Bay City.

Soot, Sparks and Snake Heads, Early Travel Was No Picnic

The Michigan Central arrives at Dearborn in 1838.

Mayor Bingham, repair agent for the Erie and Kalamazoo Railroad, stepped aboard the train at Palmyra, a Lenawee County hamlet. It was a December afternoon in 1841, a nasty day during which freezing rain had coated everything with a layer of ice.

The train, one of only three or four in the state, consisted of a diminutive locomotive capable of making about 10 miles per hour on the downgrade, a fuel tender stacked high with cordwood and one passenger coach containing three compartments. A caboose would have been superfluous had it even been invented.

Spying some acquaintances, Bingham joined them in the middle compartment. He passed up an adjoining seat because its cushion was out of place, instead seated himself behind, facing the front of the train. The locomotive's two drive wheels spun on the icy track, its huge smokestack spewed a mixture of black smoke, soot and glowing coals and the train was off for the six-mile run to Adrian.

The tracks of this first railroad to be operated west of Schenectady, N.Y., were wood rails on which had been spiked lengths of strap iron five-eighths of an inch thick and 2½ inches wide. The vibrations of the passing train sometimes caused the short spikes to work loose and the strap iron to curl up like a giant spring, producing a dreaded "snake head."

Bingham's train had gotten less than a half-mile from Palmyra when suddenly a snake head crashed into the bottom of the coach up through the seat he had rejected. It caught him under the chin, smashing him through the partition behind.

Luckily, the entire section of strap iron broke loose to be dragged along by the train. Bingham came to with his head and shoulders sticking through the partition. Because he had grasped the snake head in his hands and wore a thick scarf he had been spared from serious injury. He helped the engineer and fireman respike the rail in place, and the train continued on to Adrian, having made the 33-mile run from Toledo in 10 hours.

Bingham and fellow passengers fared little better during the return trip the next morning. When the locomotive ran out of wood and water everybody alighted to glean sticks from the woods and dip water from the ditches. It ran out again about four miles from Toledo. The passengers left the "jerkwater" standing on the tracks and hiked the rest of the way. Such were the pitfalls of pioneer train travel.

Construction of America's first passenger line, the Baltimore and Ohio, had begun in 1828. Despite fears by clergymen that trains would somehow lower morality, Michigan was soon caught up in the railroad fever. By 1830 the Territorial Council had granted a charter to the Pontiac and Detroit Railway. But that line never developed beyond the planning stage.

On April 22, 1833, entrepreneurs from Adrian secured a charter for a railroad intended to link Port Lawrence, later renamed Toledo, with the headwaters of the Kalamazoo River. Despite the Toledo War, which resulted in the Toledo strip, including Port Lawrence, being awarded to Ohio, the laying of the wooden rail to Adrian proceeded rapidly.

On November 2, 1836, Adrian greeted the arrival of the Erie and Kalamazoo's first horse-drawn coach with a gala celebration featuring a parading militia unit and booming cannon. The following year the tracks had been "improved" with strap iron and a steam locomotive, the Adrian, had supplanted equine power. Unfortunately, the first top-heavy "pleasure car," which resembled an overgrown stagecoach, frequently jumped the tracks.

After Michigan's admittance into the Union on January 26, 1837, the State Legislature launched an ambitious internal improvements program which featured several canals and three railroads across the peninsula. The southern route would link Monroe with New Buffalo, the central route Detroit with St. Joseph, and the northern route St. Clair with the Grand River. By January 1838 the 28-mile section of the central route between Detroit and Dearborn had been completed and the following month a locomotive chugged into Ypsilanti.

The southern route west of Adrian ran into political problems, however. Various settlements in Lenawee and Hillsdale counties vied to divert the path of the railroad. The easiest and most direct route to Hillsdale would have passed through the Lenawee County town of Keene. However, Lanesville, later renamed Hudson, advocates succeeded through political intrigue and financial allurements to cause the route to be kinked three miles through rough terrain to their village. A number of Keene merchants accepted the inevitable by relocating to Lanesville. One even jacked up his hotel and had it pulled there by oxen.

The national depression which hit Michigan in 1838 brought a temporary halt to the state's grandiose plans for internal improvements. However, the line that would become the Michigan Central reached Jackson by 1842, and Marshall two years later. On Sunday February 1, 1846, Kalamazoo congregations emptied churches when they heard the steam whistle of the first locomotive. Both the Michigan Central and the Michigan Southern finally reached Chicago in 1852.

Copper Fever

A Keweenaw miner chisels at a vein of solid copper.

Robert E. Clarke, an eastern journalist touring Michigan's Copper Country during the summer of 1852, surveyed the village of Eagle River in puzzlement. Most of the 20 to 30 houses huddled along the bluff on the west side of the Keweenaw Peninsula sported high flag poles. They reminded Clarke of the naked masts of sailing vessels in harbor. He soon learned their real function.

The structures doubled as taverns, or "groceries" as they were euphemistically called. Each Sunday, gaudy pennants advertising the relative merits of the groceries flapped high in the breeze, beckoning the area's many miners. There, they spent their only day of rest quaffing tumblers of "forty-rod," a potent potable reputedly able to knock over a greenhorn at 40 rods by its smell alone.

Forty-rod fit well the tough breed of men who flocked to the rugged Copper Country in the 1840s. Although rumors of huge nuggets of native copper had circulated for centuries, it took the documented reports of Michigan's first state geologist, Douglass Houghton, and the excitement generated by the exhibition of the "Ontonagon boulder" in 1843 to catch the nation's fancy. The icy waters of Lake Superior near Eagle River ended 36-year-old Houghton's promising career in 1845, but not before he had witnessed a frenzied rush for red metal that rivaled the '49ers' later dash for California gold.

The native Chippewa ceded rights to some 25,000 square miles of land west of Marquette at the Treaty of La Pointe in 1842. The following spring, the first vessel out of the Sault carried Captain Walter Cunningham, who promptly opened a federal mineral land agency at the new settlement of Copper Harbor. The vessel also carried about 20 prospectors, the beginnings of a torrent of copper hunters that ultimately numbered in the thousands.

Hordes of adventurers who knew little or nothing about prospecting left comfortable homes down below to seek fortunes in the Keweenaw wilderness. Copper Harbor, Eagle Harbor, Ontonagon, and the other boom towns that sprang up also attracted a motley lot of loose ladies, gamblers and con men equally eager to make a go of it. A specialized variety of barfly known as "white Pawnees" because they bought legitimate prospectors drinks and pawed them in mock friendship, cajoled the location of promising strikes and then rushed to claim adjoining tracts.

Michigan's Copper Country is one of the only places on earth where large nuggets of pure copper occur. At first, those big nuggets were the only prizes the copper hunters would settle for. Fighting swarms of black flies and mosquitoes, soon dubbed "Keweenaw eagles," prospectors stumbled through the thick forests and splashed through the peninsula's many swamps, hunting native copper boulders or outcroppings. Most found some copper, but rarely enough to make a profit.

When large masses of copper were discovered, they needed to be laboriously chiseled into manageable pieces. Transportation costs, which included unloading at the Sault for a trip around the rapids on a primitive horse-drawn railroad, were prohibitively high.

By 1846 approximately 1,000 leases, originally 9 miles square but soon reduced to one square mile in size, had been granted. Few were ever actually worked. A lively trade in lease permits developed and some speculators made small fortunes without lifting a shovel. Charles Lanman, who visited the region in 1846, estimated that at least 500 men in Copper Harbor alone were engaged in permit speculation.

In May of that year, however, President James K. Polk suspended further issuance of permits. Despite the promise of rich finds such as the Cliff Mine - reputedly discovered the hard way when a prospector's soft bottom encountered a sharp chunk of copper as he slid down a stone bluff - by late 1847 the speculative bubble had burst. Most of the red-metal hunters returned to civilization, poorer but wiser men.

Some who lingered in the north country, however, made spectacular finds. A favorite prospecting method was to search for old pits excavated by prehistoric miners, sites that sometimes contained workable lodes of copper. Sam Knapp, a former Vermont tavern keeper, had come to the Ontonagon wilderness in 1844, curiously enough, for health reasons. Four years later, he stumbled upon a large depression in a forest clearing that looked promising. He shoveled through a deep mantle of snow to find the opening of a man-made cavern.

As he and companions began removing centuries of accumulated debris from the hole, they uncovered scores of stone hammers and other ancient mining tools. Beneath the rubble lay a large mass of native copper resting on a platform of rotted logs, evidently a pre-historic attempt to raise the huge copper nugget. Better yet, at the bottom of the mine was a vein of solid copper five feet wide.

Knapp's discovery gave rise to one of the richest and most profitable copper mines in history, the legendary Minesota Mine, misspelled through a clerical error. Nearby excavations unearthed other lodes, including the largest chunk of solid copper ever found, over 500 tons in weight.

By 1855 when the Sault Canal opened, Michigan was producing more copper than any other state in the Union. The famous Calumet and Hecla Mine, discovered when some runaway pigs tumbled into another prehis-toric pit, went into operation in 1864. Ultimately more than 13 billion pounds of copper came from the region awarded to Michigan as compensation for its loss of the Toledo strip!

"Boys, Look Around and See What You Can Find!": The Discovery of Iron Ore in the U.P.

William Austin Burt's survey team near Teal Lake in 1844.

In all his many years of surveying, William Austin Burt had never seen the magnetic compass act like it did September 19, 1844.

Burt and seven assistants were running the first survey of the Upper Peninsula mineral region. The evening before, they had camped on the east side of Teal Lake, approximately 12 miles west of the present site of Marquette. When they continued their survey west in the morning, the compass needle seemed absolutely bewitched. At one location it pointed due west; at another, due east; and in some places, it dipped to the bottom of the box and would not revolve in any direction.

Burt was able to chart these abnormal fluctuations through the use of his own ingenious invention called the solar compass. It relied upon the sun's fixed position at a given latitude, longitude and time to determine true north. This day's reading fully vindicated its usefulness. "How could they survey this country without my compass?" he chortled. "What could be done here without my compass?"

Suddenly, Harvey Mellen, the compass man, called out, "Come and see a variation that will beat all." The crew gathered around the instrument to watch the north end of the needle waver between the south and west points. "Boys," Burt shouted, "look around and see what you can find!" They scattered and soon returned with specimens of iron ore. Although they probably did not then realize the full extent of their find, Burt and his survey crew had just discovered the vast deposit of high-grade iron ore that would come to be known as the Marquette Range.

Unlike some government surveyors who took advantage of their knowledge to purchase the choicest tracts, neither Burt nor any of his men capitalized on their discovery. Burt's first official report of the survey, released in 1846, noted that the iron region of the Upper Peninsula "far exceeds any other portion of the United

States in the abundance and good qualities of its iron ores."

In the meantime, however, a group of prospectors from Jackson had discovered the same iron lode. The copper fever that sent hordes of speculators to the Keweenaw country in the early 1840s had motivated a Jackson storekeeper named Philo Everett and a group of his neighbors to organize the Jackson Mining Company in the spring of 1845. Everett's company received seven federal mineral lease permits through the influence of former U.S. Senator John Norvell of Detroit, who had been instrumental in securing the western portion of the U.P. as compensation for the loss of the Toledo Strip when Michigan entered the Union in 1837.

On June 20, 1845, Everett and three other company members left Jackson for the long journey to the U.P. mining frontier. At the Sault, they hired Louis Nolan, a French fur trader, to guide them along Lake Superior's rugged southern coast to Copper Harbor. Nolan, who evidently had gotten wind of Burt's iron ore discovery, told the Jackson men that they did not need to go all the way to Copper Harbor for ore. Although Everett's party was in search of copper, mention of a mountain of ore, of a type Nolan could not identify, intrigued them. Nolan led them to the Teal Lake vicinity, but they could not find the iron deposits.

Discouraged, they began pushing on toward Copper Harbor. But, en route, they chanced upon the wigwam of a Chippewa chief named Marji-Gesick. He knew of the mountain of iron ore. It was, in fact, a place held in superstitious regard by the local Indians. The chief agreed to guide them there, but he would not personally venture into this domain of the evil spirits.

When they arrived at the hill of iron, the chief pointed toward the uprooted stump of an ancient white pine. There, two of Everett's party found chunks of high-grade iron ore clinging to the roots. Everett soon entered a mining claim to a one-square-mile tract near the present site of Negaunee. The Jackson Mining Company rewarded Marji-Gesick with a hastily scrawled-out note entitling him to twelve-one-hundredths of the company's interest in the claim.

Everett returned triumphantly to Jackson with ore samples he described as "bright as a bar of iron just broken." The ore was so rich, in fact, that when iron-workers using technology adapted to inferior ore tried to smelt it and could not, they pronounced it worthless.

But the Jackson Mining Co. refused to accept that setback. In 1846, another expedition to the site brought back additional specimens of ore. Everett took the ore to a foundry located at a Branch County hamlet later known as Hodunk. The ironmaster there succeeded in smelting the first iron from U.P. ore. Everett had the bar of iron converted into fine steel at a Jackson forge and a piece made into a prize knife blade.

In the summer of 1847, the company built a forge about three miles from the Jackson Mine on Carp River, where on February 10, 1848, they produced the first iron in the Lake Superior country. The daily output was about six tons of four-inch-square by two-foot-long "blooms" of iron. But the difficulty of transporting iron bars over 10 miles of miserable roads to Marquette, the expense of securing sufficient charcoal for the furnaces, and other problems made the forging of iron in the Upper Peninsula a losing proposition. Not until the opening of the Sault Canal in 1855 made it possible to transport iron ore to eastern furnaces economically could money be made from Lake Superior iron. Despite their pioneering efforts, the original members of the Jackson Mining Co. made little money on their venture.

Marji-Gesick also failed to receive anything for his services. After he had died in poverty, however, his daughter Charlotte found the document entitling him to a share in the mine. She proved its validity in a famous trial decided before the Michigan Supreme Court, which provided the plot for Robert Traver's (John Voelker) popular novel, *Laughing Whitefish*.

The iron-ore dock at Marquette, ca. 1873.

Fort Wilkins, Where Time Stood Still

Fort Wilkins, ca. 1850.

The four infantry companies stood stiffly at attention on the parade ground at Fort Wilkins as the Stars and Stripes rose. Behind the tall flagpole lapped the tranquil waters of Lake Fanny Hooe mirroring the massive red pine and cedar that crowded its shores.

It was the morning of August 30, 1845, and the American flag that flapped in the breeze carried only 27 stars, the last having been added when Florida entered the Union six months before. But those infantrymen then assembled in the remote fort at the tip of the Keweenaw Peninsula would soon participate in military campaigns that would dramatically enhance their nation's geographic dimensions and the number of stars on its flag. They would not battle wild northern tribesmen or unruly copper miners, fears of whom had motivated the U.S. government to establish Fort Wilkins, but Mexican armies south of the Rio Grande.

The men of companies A and B, 5th U.S. Infantry, who had constructed the fort the previous summer, would, in fact, leave that day for the long journey down the lakes to Detroit, and from there join Gen. Zachary Taylor's army poised at the Texas border. Companies I and K of the 2nd U.S. Infantry, who had arrived to replace them two weeks before, would continue to garrison the fort until they too were assigned to Taylor's army in 1846. Twenty-one years would pass before the army saw fit to re-garrison Fort Wilkins.

In the interim, many of the soldiers who had been stationed there in 1845 would distinguish themselves. Capt. William Alburtis made the supreme sacrifice for his country at the siege of Vera Cruz, Mexico, in March 1847. Lt. Charles S. Hamilton fought in five battles during the Mexican War and rose to the rank of major general in the Civil War. Capt. Robert Emmett Clay also served as a Union general. Lts. Daniel Ruggles and Carter Stevenson, however, rallied to the Southern cause and both ultimately became Confederate major generals.

For those officers and most of their men, duty at Fort Wilkins had been a vexing interruption to their military careers. Lt. Stevenson's friends, for example, had successfully petitioned President John Tyler to intervene in his transfer to Fort Wilkins, but unable to find a substitute he reluctantly accompanied his unit there. Two privates, however, deserted in Detroit rather than serve in the northern wilderness.

Lt. Hamilton, who was a member of the second contingent that arrived in the summer of 1845, was concerned about losing out on the glories of Mexican battles. Hoping for a speedy transfer, he purchased Spanish books in Detroit and studied that language during the long Keweenaw winter he spent cooped up at Fort Wilkins. He later bitterly wrote, "There was no need of a military force being stationed there, but the then-Secretary of War, Wilkins. desired to immortalize himself and ordered a post erected which, in honor of himself, was called Fort Wilkins."

Actually, Michigan's senators and representatives had drawn up, on March 15, 1844, a petition asking for the establishment of a fort in the Copper Country and presented it to Secretary of War William Wilkins of Pennsylvania. Their main concern had been the possibility of an Indian uprising aggravated by the hordes of prospectors who had rushed for the copper bonanza. Illegal encroachments on federal lands by the miners may have been a secondary motive. Neither threat ever amounted to much.

Nevertheless, Wilkins and General in Chief of the U.S. Army Winfield Scott approved of the measure and ordered two companies of the 5th Regiment to proceed from Detroit to the Copper Country and erect a fort. The soldiers reached Copper Harbor on May 27, 1844, and selected a site just south of that settlement, bordering the north side of a narrow inland lake. Lt. Ruggles later named it Fanny Hooe in honor of his sister-in-law, who spent a summer with the regiment.

With the assistance of ten "citizen mechanics," the troops quarried foundation stones from nearby outcroppings, cut and squared red pine logs with broadaxes and adzes and raised the frames of 16 structures. Sharpened log palisades surrounded the fort to the shore of Lake Fanny Hooe. Windows, lumber, shingles, cut nails and plaster were shipped from Detroit. On November 15, 1844, Capt. Clary reported that "the buildings of this post are with slight exceptions, completed, and we have now as good and as comfortable quarters as any in the service." Those buildings included separate quarters for officers, enlisted men and married enlisted personnel, two company kitchens and messrooms, a bakery, hospital, guardhouse, quartermaster's warehouse, sutler's store, stables, slaughterhouse, icehouse, workshops for blacksmiths and carpenters and a powder magazine.

In addition to construction work, the troops cut a supply of firewood, sufficient, they hoped, for the long winter, and planted a vegetable garden. The garden failed that first year but the following summer a more fertile plot located near the west end of Lake Fanny Hooe brought better results.

With the exception of some game and fish, all the garrison's winter rations had to be delivered by one of the two supply ships then on Lake Superior. Unfortunately, the largest, the John Jacob Astor, was torn to pieces on the jagged rocks at Copper Harbor during a terrific gale that September. The schooner Algonquin managed to convey sufficient supplies to the fort before winter sealed it off. However, all but 25 of 607 bushels of potatoes were condemned upon arrival, 23 out of 40 barrels of pork were found to be rotten, and the entire lot of vinegar, a 19th century culinary necessity, was "in bad taste."

Lousy chow was but one of the problems the soldiers faced that winter. Entertainment for the snowbound and incommunicado garrison consisted of keeping warm and an occasional game of cards or checkers. Not surprisingly, some of the soldiers managed to get their hands on a supply of liquor, 250 gallons to be exact. But following a rousing fistfight in one of the barracks, their secret was discovered and officers seized the forbidden potable and presumably destroyed it.

Several of the officers had wives with them, but even they suffered the effects of cabin fever. By spring, there were "scarcely any two officers on speaking terms."

Infrequent mail service posed another problem. Whatever mail made its way to the fort did so via dog sled. Lt. Hamilton first learned that he had been promoted and assigned to duty in Texas effective November 1845 when mail arrived the following February. He was unable to leave until May.

The rest of his unit also vacated the fort in July 1846. A solitary sergeant was left in charge of the facility. Following the Civil War the Army again garrisoned the fort in 1867, then abandoned it permanently on August 30, 1870. The Fort Wilkins reservation was soon transferred to the Department of Interior and in 1892 to the U.S. Lighthouse Board. Houghton and Keweenaw counties purchased the grounds in 1921 and, two years later, deeded the property to the State of Michigan for park purposes.

Although it was actually one of the least significant forts in American history, reconstructed Fort Wilkins today offers tourists a peep back into time at life on a frontier army post of the 1840s.

Who Killed
James Schoolcraft?

John Tanner, a "damn mean Injun?"

James Schoolcraft had long been an embarrassment to his respectable older brother, Henry. His drunken, rakish ways shocked even the notoriously tough frontier town of Sault Ste. Marie. Few locals were surprised when he took advantage of his wife's maternity absence to celebrate Independence Day 1846 by canoeing across the St. Marys River to Sault, Canada for a wild spree.

Still suffering the effects of his carousal, Schoolcraft rose about noon the next day. He stepped into a pair of slippers and sauntered down the path that led to his garden plot.

Suddenly from the heavy underbrush alongside the path, a muzzle boomed. A one-inch musket ball and three buckshots, cut through his heart. Schoolcraft leaped forward out of his slippers and fell to the ground, dead.

Two boys clearing brush nearby heard the shot and saw a puff of gun smoke. But when they ran to the murder scene all they found were Schoolcraft's body and his slippers sitting side by side in the path behind. Later investigators found one more bit of evidence, a tightly crumpled piece of paper, evidently used as wadding for the musket load. It proved to be a leaf from a hymn book used at the local Baptist chapel.

Who killed James Schoolcraft? Opinion quickly focused on the Sault's resident wild man, John Tanner, remembered by one acquaintance as a "damn mean Injun."

Tanner, in fact, was a white man who had been raised by the Indians. At the age of nine he had been spirited away from his Kentucky homestead by a pair of marauding Chippewa from the Saginaw Valley. They sold him to an Ottawa squaw from northern Michigan who raised him as her son. Eventually they migrated west to Manitoba. Tanner became a celebrated hunter, resembling his fellow tribesmen in every way but skin color.

After 30 years of life among the Indians, Tanner returned to civilization in 1819 to seek out his lost relatives. He determined to stay, and the following year he brought his Indian wife and children to Mackinac Island. By 1828 he had learned enough English to secure a job as interpreter for Henry Schoolcraft, Indian agent at the Sault. But Schoolcraft soon fired him. Tanner apparently was mentally ill, subject to uncontrollable fits of rage and destruction. When in ugly moods, he so mistreated his family that the Michigan Territorial Legislature passed an act in 1830 authorizing the sheriff of Chippewa County to remove his daughter, Martha, to a place of refuge.

After Schoolcraft dismissed him, the Rev. Abel Bingham, Baptist missionary to the Sault, hired Tanner as an interpreter. But even the minister was unable to tolerate his periodic frenzies. Tanner, it seems, had also learned the Indian custom of seeking violent revenge against those he thought had wronged him or his kin. He repeatedly threatened to get even with Schoolcraft, Bingham and several other prominent Sault residents.

The night before James Schoolcraft's murder, Tanner's house mysteriously burned to the ground. Search parties found no trace of Tanner, but as residents later recalled, they never ventured too far into the woods. For months the spectre of the wild man returning to complete his revenge haunted the community. Dead livestock, forest fires and missing persons were blamed on Tanner. Rumors circulated of a strange white man living among the Indians of the far north, but Tanner was never positively seen again.

In their excitement during what old-timers long remembered as the "Tanner summer," hardly anyone considered another suspect in the Schoolcraft murder case. Apparently, during his revelry on the Fourth of July, Schoolcraft had gotten into an altercation over a woman with Lt. Bryant P. Tilden, an officer at Fort

Brady. Witnesses heard Tilden remark that "cold lead would settle it."

Shortly after the murder, most of the Fort Brady garrison served in the Mexican War under General Winfield Scott. News reached the Sault that Tilden had been court-martialed for murder and burglary in Mexico and sentenced to be hung. His sentence, however, was remitted. He resigned his commission in 1848 and served as a geologist until his death in 1859. Tanner's daughter, Martha, maintained that Tilden confessed to the crime on his deathbed.

Some Sault residents were troubled by another bizarre set of circumstances. On the afternoon of the murder, two soldiers returned from what they claimed was a hunting expedition. The musket of one had been fired. Schoolcraft had been killed by the standard military-issue "buck and ball" load.

About a month later, while standing with a group of soldiers before the gates of the fort, both men were struck dead by a bolt of lightning!

The Train-Boy
From Michigan

Thomas Edison at the age of 14.

The conductor called "All Aboooard," signaled to the engineer, and with a hiss of released steam the wheels of the Grand Trunk locomotive slowly began to revolve. Suddenly, the running feet of a little ragamuffin thrummed the wooden platform of the Smith Creek station in St. Clair County.

Hugging big bales of Detroit Free Press newspapers under each arm, he leaped for the door of the freight car. But he lost his balance and began to topple backwards, perhaps to roll under the wheels of the train. The conductor reached out and grabbed the only thing he could reach, the boys ears, and yanked him aboard. Young Thomas Edison felt "something crack inside" his head. The life of the 12-year-old had been saved, but from that moment on he never again "heard a bird sing."

Born February 11, 1847, in Milan, Ohio, Thomas Alva Edison never seemed quite like the other boys. His head was so abnormally large at birth that the village doctor feared he had "brain fever." As soon as he could talk he began asking questions about everything around him. "Why does the goose squat on the eggs?" he asked his mother. "To keep them warm so they'll hatch," she replied. Later that day, his father found him "curled up in a nest he had made in the barn filled with goose and chicken eggs."

At the age of six, he started a little fire in the same barn "just to see what it would do," and the structure burned to the ground. He had so much trouble in school, always ending up "at the foot of the class," that his mother, a former school teacher, began instructing him at home.

In 1854, when the Milan economy went sour, the Edison family moved to the booming Michigan lumber town of Port Huron. They rented a large house on the Fort Gratiot reserve at the northern edge of town. There, Edison continued his youthful experimentation.

To the dismay of two big tomcats, he tied their tails to a wire and tried to produce static electricity by rubbing their fur vigorously. A playmate fared even worse. Edison convinced him to swallow a large dose of an effervescent remedy called Seidlitz powders so that the gas produced might make him fly through the air like a balloon. His friend got good and sick, and the experimenter earned a thrashing.

By the time he was 10, Edison had developed a passion for chemistry. He spent all his pocket money on chemicals, which he arranged in hundreds of bottles in a basement laboratory. There, he spent endless hours tinkering with wet-cell batteries and other magical apparatus. He also strung up a line of stovepipe wire and built his own primitive telegraph set.

In 1859, the Grand Trunk railroad reached Port Huron. Motivated by a need for more money to buy scientific equipment as well as his family's poverty, the 11-year-old got a job as a "candy butcher." At 6:30 each morning he climbed aboard the train and hawked apples, peanuts, candy and newspapers to passengers during the three-hour run to Detroit. He made good use of the six-hour layover to read his way through most of the Detroit Public Library. The return trip landed him back in Port Huron at 9:30 p.m., with no time to continue his beloved scientific experimentation.

So, Edison talked the trainman into letting him install his laboratory in an unused section of the baggage car. The young entrepreneur also acquired a printing outfit and published the little *Weekly Herald* on the train. It contained bits of national news, railroad gossip and his own philosophical editorials. All went well until a bad section of track caused a piece of phosphorus to jar loose from its water-filled bottle. The chemical ignited and set the baggage car on fire. Edison's laboratory and printing press were unceremoniously ejected at the next station.

Undaunted, Edison moved his press back home, where he published an enlarged version of the paper called *Paul Pry*. In tune with its title, *Paul Pry* featured society news and town gossip. One scandalous piece so infuriated a local citizen that when he chanced upon the young editor near the Port Huron docks he pitched him into the river. Edison lost interest in the newspaper business about that time.

In the summer of 1862, Edison, in true Horatio Alger style, pulled the three-year-old son of the Mt. Clemens stationmaster from the path of a boxcar. The grateful father rewarded the hero by training him to be a telegraph operator. Despite his partial deafness, Edison could distinguish the clicks of the telegraph key. Following a five-month apprenticeship, he launched a career as a railroad telegrapher. In 1864, he left his first position in Port Huron to bounce around the midwest to Adrian, Fort Wayne, Indianapolis and Cincinnati. All the while he continued to experiment and invent.

In 1868, while in Boston, he secured his first patent for a telegraphic vote-recording machine. That proved a commercial failure, but ultimately Edison's other inventions, including the electric light bulb, phonograph and motion-picture camera and projector, revolutionized society.

During his funeral in 1931, the nation dimmed its lights in honor of the train-boy from Michigan.

Doctor Chase and the
Case of the Canal-Boat
Cook

Dr. Alvin Chase of Ann Arbor, who was trusted by millions.

Dr. Alvin Chase stroked his beard in a wise professional manner as he considered the case of the canal-boat cook.

The Ann Arbor physician and compiler of a popular collection of home remedies, cooking recipes and other trade secrets was traveling on a mule-drawn canal boat in western Pennsylvania. It was shortly after supper when it happened. The cook came down with a terrific stomach ache. Her husband, the steersman, had looked in vain for the usual remedy in such cases, peppermint and whiskey.

As her moans grew louder, he appealed to Chase for help. The doctor "ran his mind" over the various medicines he had on hand. No, nothing for a stomach ache - but wait, what about the Magnetic Tooth Cordial? Why, it had given such "decided relief" to the suffering sheriff of Wayne County, Indiana, that he had handed Chase an entire $3 piece saying, "Take whatever you please."

The problem with the cordial, a tincture of opium, chloroform, gum camphor, oil of cloves, sulphuric ether and oil of lavender, was that it was intended to be applied externally. But, reasoned Chase, if it was good for external pains, why not for internal as well? He measured a teaspoonful of the mixture into a tumbler of water and gave it to his patient to drink. Five minutes passed and still she groaned in pain. The doctor then decided to "go whole hog or none" and gave her another dose. Miraculously, within another five minutes she was "perfectly cured."

The patient's grateful husband, the other steersman and one of the mule drivers soon handed a dollar over to the doctor for his book, *Information For Everybody*, containing recipes for several hundred similar remedies. Chase described his wonderful success in curing the canal-boat cook in succeeding editions and also changed the name of the remedy to the "Magnetic

Tooth Cordial and Pain Killer."

Beginning in the 1850s and continuing well into the 20th century, millions of Americans counted Chase's book second in importance only to the Bible and in the process made the good doctor's name a household word from coast to coast.

Born in Cayuga County, New York in 1817, Chase took to the road at the age of 17 as an itinerant peddler, centering his operations in northern Ohio and Michigan. As he wandered he collected recipes for tasty dishes, better ways of making things and especially nostrums for whatever ailed man or beast. Somewhere along the line, Chase decided that his true calling was that of a physician.

He settled down in Ann Arbor in 1856 and began taking medical classes at the University of Michigan. Unable to graduate from that prestigious institution because he lacked a background in Latin or natural history, he enrolled in the Eclectic Medical Institute in Cincinnati in 1858. By studying 16 hours a day he earned his medical diploma in four months and graduated as class valedictorian as well.

As their name implied, eclectic practitioners freely chose from the remedies advocated by the diverse medical theories then in vogue. They sometimes, in fact, let the patient, or next of kin, choose the treatment.

Following graduation, Chase hung out his shingle in Ann Arbor. He augmented the poor earnings common to general practitioners of that era by continuing to peddle his recipe books. Each succeeding edition grew more comprehensive. By 1860, the eighth edition contained 600 recipes. Three years later, he had added 200 more recipes to the tenth and most popular edition.

In 1864, he began construction of his own printing establishment, an Italianate structure still standing at the corner of Miller and Main streets. Four years later, as sales of *Dr. Chase's Recipes Or Information For Every-body* boomed, he tripled the size of the building. He kept 50 typesetters, pressmen, binders and other artisans busy making his books.

Although there is undoubtedly much good old-fashioned folk wisdom locked within the book's pages, many of Dr. Chase's recipes seem a mite peculiar by modern standards. For example, among the 11 cures offered for ague, as malaria was then called, can be found soot coffee, made by steeping one tablespoon of soot scraped from a chimney in a pint of hot water. Another of Chase's ague cures, sent from the spirit world via a clairvoyant, called for various herbs to be dissolved in a gallon of "best rye whisky." The dosage of five or six wine glasses full per day must certainly have at least brightened up the sick room.

A kindly old Dutch woman supplied Chase with her favorite no-fail remedy for the croup - a teaspoon of urine and goose grease taken every 15 minutes until well. Nearly as repulsive was Chase's remedy for sprains - toad ointment. It was made by boiling four large toads until quite soft and adding the resulting liquid to butter.

Then there was the case, Chase cited, of the Hoosier couple troubled with "piles." The missus cured herself by sitting in warm water, while her mate achieved the same success with cold water. True to his eclectic training, Chase provided many other contradictory cures with the rationale, "If one fails, a remedy may certainly be found amongst the many others given." If you survived the first experiments, that is.

Among Chase's practical suggestions for staying healthy is his advice to women - exercise. He thought hoeing in the garden, sweeping and dusting the best such exercises for the fair sex.

In addition to medical advice for humans, Chase offered many similar cures for animals. His book also contained sections with practical advice for merchants and grocers, saloon keepers, tanners, painters, blacksmiths, tinners, gunsmiths, jewelers, cabinetmakers and other artisans. His cookery section taught how to make the best cakes, pies, puddings and other dishes, which he had sampled during his many travels. A barbers' and toilet department carried no less than eight "sure fire" hair restoratives, sufficient to make an Upjohn chemist green with envy.

By 1869 Chase had sold approximately 500,000 copies of his book. That year, he sold out to Rice A. Beal, agreeing never to go back into the recipe business in Michigan. He moved to Sauk Rapids, Minnesota, in an effort to regain his failing health.

Three years later and rejuvenated, Chase was back in Ann Arbor attempting to market another book titled *Dr. Chase's Family, Physician, Farrier, Beekeeper, And Second Book Of Recipes.* But Beal soon won a suit against the doctor, and Chase moved his operation to Toledo. Somehow, Chase's backers got control of the business and when the smoke cleared he had lost all his money. Meanwhile, the two rival firms continued a land office business in the sale of his books.

Chase died in 1885. Within weeks, still another publisher in Detroit brought out a "memorial edition" of his third book. By 1931 when the various editions were consolidated into one mammoth volume, an estimated four million copies of Chase's recipe books had been sold.

As to the effectiveness of the various medical recipes Chase had collected - caveat emptor. Consider the unfortunate fact that Chase's wife and five children, whom he often used as guinea pigs for new remedies, all preceded him in death.

Old Zach,
Radical Republican

Senator Zachariah Chandler, radical Republican leader.

Sen. Zachariah Chandler clenched his goateed jaw as he watched the long line of bluecoats scramble along the Warrenton Turnpike away from the First Battle of Bull Run. He had helped bring on the conflict by writing a much publicized letter to Michigan Governor Austin Blair in which he had declared "without a little blood-letting this Union will not, in my estimation, be worth a rush." But he little expected this first major battle of the Civil War to result in a disastrous Union rout.

Chandler, five other U.S. senators, 10 representatives and a crowd of civilians, including gaily bedecked Washington belles, had ridden out to the hills west of Washington on the afternoon of July 21, 1861 to observe the clash between Union Gen. Irwin McDowell's and Confederate Gen. P.G.T. Beauregard's armies. Their pleasant Sunday outing had turned sour when they saw the road fill with retreating Union soldiers. The stream of civilian carriages worsened the traffic snarl and when a Confederate shell scored a direct hit on a wagon, thereby blocking the bridge over Cub Run, the retreat turned into a panic. The curses of army teamsters mingled with the screams of horror-stricken ladies.

Chandler, Sen. Benjamin Wade and several representatives had tried to stop the retreat by standing in the road with raised pistols and even grabbing the bits of horses, but to little avail. Muddy and tired, Chandler arrived back at Washington late that night. He rushed to the White House to buoy up despondent President Lincoln. He urged Lincoln "to show to the country and the rebels that the government was not discouraged a whit, but was just beginning to get mad." His timely counsel helped restore the president's resolution to prosecute the war.

Chandler was born in Bedford, New Hampshire on December 10, 1813. When he reached 20 his father offered him a choice of a college education or $1,000 cash. He chose the latter and in 1834 immigrated to Detroit where he opened a dry goods store with his brother-in-law, Franklin Moore. By the mid 1840s Chandler's firm had become the largest of its type in the state and he a wealthy man.

Soon, he threw his hat in the political ring, serving first as a Detroit alderman. In 1851 he was elected mayor on the Whig ticket. He ran as Whig candidate for governor in 1852 but was defeated. He became an ardent anti-slavery advocate and took an active role in the formation of the Republican Party "under the oaks" in Jackson in 1854. Three years later, Chandler won election to the senate seat vacated when Lewis Cass became James Buchanan's secretary of state. He held that position for the next 18 years, becoming one of the most powerful senators in Washington.

In 1858, Chandler made his first important speech, against the admittance of Kansas into the Union under the pro-slavery Le Compton Constitution. He became one of the leaders of the anti-slavery, no-compromise-with-the-South faction. South Carolina's secession, the formation of the Confederate government, and lame duck President Buchanan's stance that the federal government had no power to prevent secession by force, spurred him to write his "blood letter" to Governor Blair on February 11, 1861. It further inflamed Southern hot heads, the situation deteriorated, and with the bombardment of Fort Sumter on April 12 the Civil War began.

Throughout the war, Chandler remained a firm friend of Lincoln. In July 1862, he risked political suicide by delivering a vehement speech against popular General George B. McClellan. Chandler, however, in concert with other so-called radical Republicans championed a harsher policy toward the South than Lincoln felt necessary. Nevertheless, Chandler actively campaigned for his friend during the election of 1864.

Andrew Johnson, who succeeded Lincoln following the assassination of the president on April 14, 1865, advocated a similar lenient reconstruction policy for the defeated Confederate states. Chandler and other radical Republicans passed punitive reconstruction measures over Johnson's veto. When Johnson contested the legality of the radical Republican-sponsored Tenure of Office Act by dismissing Secretary of War Edwin Stanton, the house impeached him. Chandler took an active role in the subsequent impeachment trial in the Senate. Johnson won acquittal by one vote, which Chandler considered "one of the most bitter disappointments of his political career."

By 1875, Chandler's partiality toward friends, especially in securing lucrative government positions, brought a reaction by younger up-and-coming Michigan Republicans. "Chandlerism" became a pejorative term and he was defeated in his bid for reelection. President Ulysses S. Grant, however, soon appointed "Old Zach" Secretary of the Interior.

In 1879, Isaac P. Christiancy, who had assumed Chandler's senatorial seat, resigned. The Michigan Legislature promptly elected Chandler to fill the vacancy. He soon made national headlines again by "waving the bloody flag." He delivered a blustering speech in the Senate denouncing Jefferson Davis, who was being considered for a pension for his military services prior to the war.

Chandler felt he had a good chance to win the Republican nomination for the upcoming presidential election. But when he went to Chicago to deliver a political speech on October 31, 1879, he was found dead in his hotel room the next morning. In 1913, Michigan installed a large marble statue of Chandler in Statuary Hall of the U.S. Capitol Building. "Old Zach" and Lewis Cass are the only Michiganians to have been so honored.

Franklin Thompson, Female Soldier

Sarah Edmonds, alias Pvt. Franklin Thompson.

"Take that black rascal and set him to work, and if he don't work well tie him up and give him twenty lashes," the Confederate officer barked to the civilian overseer. The overseer put the slim black youth to work wheelbarrowing loads of gravel up the eight-foot embankments at Yorktown, Virginia.

Little did the Confederates realize that their new laborer was actually Pvt. Franklin Thompson of the 2nd Michigan Infantry. Union Maj. Gen. George McClellan had sent him behind enemy lines on a spy mission. Thompson had donned a set of ragged clothes, blackened his skin with silver nitrate, and covered his shaven skull with a wooly wig. So adept was Thompson at disguise, in fact, that no one, not even the men in his own unit, knew that "he" was actually a "she," - Sarah Emma Edmonds of Flint.

Born in New Brunswick, Canada in 1842 to a strict Scotch father who only wanted sons, Sarah Edmonds grew into a headstrong tomboy, skilled in riding and marksmanship. As a teenager, she ran away from home disguised as a boy to escape a marriage her father had arranged. She retained her masculine alter ego and secured a job as a salesman for a Hartford, Conn. Bible publisher.

In 1860, she moved to Flint where a friend remembered her as a "good-looking, likable, successful young man, who made money, dressed well, drove his horse and buggy, and had many lady friends."

When the Civil War broke out in 1861, Edmonds succumbed to the rampant patriotic mood and enlisted in the Flint Union Grays, which became Co. F, 2nd Michigan Infantry. Physical exams were not required at that time. She saw combat with the 2nd Michigan during the Battle of Blackburn's Ford and in covering the Union retreat following the disastrous first Battle of Bull Run.

In April 1862, she volunteered as a spy to avenge the

death of a fellow soldier and childhood friend. She was accepted following an interrogation by McClellan and staff and a cranial examination by a phrenologist which revealed highly developed bumps of secretiveness and combativeness. Her first assignment was to report on the Confederate works before Yorktown.

Disguised as a black youth, she succeeded in infiltrating the rebel lines and was soon impressed into a work detail. The first day's labor left her hands blistered and bleeding, but that night she managed to draw a map of the Confederate artillery positions. Two days later, she was handed a rifle and placed on guard duty. She slipped back into the Union lines and turned over her information along with the Confederate rifle.

Edmonds made several more daring forays behind Confederate lines during the ensuing year, masquerading as a young Confederate soldier, a dry goods clerk, a female slave, and an Irish peddler woman. When not on espionage missions, Edmonds served as brigade mail carrier and an aide to Col. Orlando Poe.

Most of her comrades never discovered her true sex. One, in fact, recalled 20 years later that "he was a whole-souled, enthusiastic youngster, frank and fearless." But one member of the 2nd Michigan, Jerome Robbins, shifted from "he" to "she" when referring to Frank in his diary entries.

When the 2nd Michigan was transferred to Kentucky in the spring of 1863 Edmonds deserted. She later claimed that she had contracted a severe fever and thus faced hospitalization and discovery. But evidence from two contemporary diaries suggests that she had fallen in love with James Reid of the 79th New York Infantry, who also resigned at that time.

In any event, Sarah Edmonds turned up in Oberlin, Ohio, resumed female attire and served as a nurse until the war's end. She also capitalized on her colorful exploits to write a semifictional account, *Nurse And*

Spy In The Union Army, that was published in 1865 by the same Hartford firm for which she had earlier sold Bibles. She donated most of the proceeds of her best seller to hospital work.

After the war, Edmonds married a childhood friend, Linus Seelye, and they moved first to Charlevoix and then to various cities across the country. In 1884, she attended a reunion of the 2nd Michigan in Flint where many of her former comrades first learned of her true identity.

The decades had altered the appearance of all of the aging veterans but hers had changed the most. One of her comrades was shocked to note that "the slender and wiry Frank Thompson of 1863 now appeared as a woman about medium height, and had grown rather stout and fleshy."

Her old chums urged Edmonds to apply for an army pension, and later that year Congress approved a $12-per-month pension for Sarah E. Seelye, alias Franklin Thompson. She died in La Porte, Texas in 1898 and was later buried in the Grand Army of the Republic section of the Washington Cemetery in Houston.

The Little Drummer Boy
of the Rappahannock

Robert Henry Hendershot, "the drummer boy of the Rappahannock."

Their comrades crouched low in the flat-bottomed boat, as three bluecoated men of the 7th Michigan Infantry poled with all their might. Confederate Minie balls whistled and plunked around the pontoon. Union artillery rounds shrieked overhead to explode amid the smoking ruins of Fredericksburg, Virginia. Robert H. Hendershot, a 13-year-old drummer boy who had fallen overboard while pushing off, clung to the boat as it crossed the icy Rappahannock River.

It was December 11, 1862. Maj. Gen. Ambrose Burnside's Army of the Potomac, 130,000 soldiers strong, was advancing from the north to attack Gen. Robert E. Lee's Army of Northern Virginia, which had dug in along a seven-mile front in the hills to the west of the city. Between the armies lay the Rappahannock River.

Union engineers had begun constructing pontoon bridges that morning, but Confederate sharpshooters in Fredericksburg had driven them off. The men of the 7th Michigan and the 19th Massachusetts had volunteered to cross the river in the remaining pontoons to silence the sharpshooters. Hendershot, a drummer assigned to the 8th Michigan, had taken part in the dangerous mission simply for the adventure. The boat to which he clung was the first to reach the opposite shore. The Confederate sharpshooters broke and ran as the 7th Michigan charged up the steep riverbank.

After accomplishing their main objective, the Union soldiers began looting and burning the city. Following their example, Hendershot set a house on fire and then waded out to the uncompleted pontoon bridge with a clock, two blankets and some other plunder. He carried the booty back to his camp, grabbed a rifle and returned across the by-then-completed bridge for some more fun. As he was leaving a "nice mansion" he had just torched, he spied a rebel armed with a double-barreled shotgun waiting in ambush.

The little soldier raised his gun and ordered the enemy to surrender. The Confederate soldier quickly dropped his weapon and raised his hands. Hendershot marched his prisoner to the river, where two soldiers suggested he deliver his prize to Gen. Burnside. They went along to vouch for him. When Burnside heard the story, he reportedly remarked "Well boy, if you keep on in this way many years you will soon be in my place," whereupon Burnside's staff raised three cheers for "the drummer boy of the Rappahannock."

They would have little else to cheer during the ensuing battle. When Burnside's men attacked Lee's position on December 13, they suffered a disastrous defeat. Two days later, the Army of the Potomac retreated back across the river having suffered 12,653 casualties. The much smaller Confederate force lost 5,306 men.

Hendershot, born in rural Moscow Township of Hillsdale County on February 27, 1849, had moved with his widowed mother to Tecumseh in Lenawee County seven years later. A headstrong little hoodlum, he was a trial to his mother during much of his childhood. He quit school at the age of 9 to work as a bootblack and newspaper boy. One day his mother caught him swinging the family cat around by the tail and boxed his ears. He retaliated by beating her with a broom.

A son-in-law came to her rescue, tied the boy up and whipped him soundly. But he got loose, grabbed a shotgun, pointed it at his brother-in-law and pulled the trigger. Fortunately it misfired. Hendershot jumped out of a window and hopped a freight train for Adrian, where he joined Rice's Circus.

When the Civil War broke out in April 1861, the runaway was living in Jackson. The patriotic mood that swept the community inspired Hendershot, to the chagrin of his neighbors, to practice the drum. He attached himself to Company C, 9th Michigan Infantry, then being formed in Jackson. The troops liked him, but Capt. Charles V. Deland did not want the runt in his command.

When the troop train left Jackson, Hendershot was a stowaway. In camp at Jeffersonville, Indiana, Deland soundly spanked him and threatened to tie him up and send him home. Hendershot then found a more willing commander in Capt. Oliver C. Rounds of Company B. Rounds soon regretted his decision. The 12-year-old obeyed nothing but his own desires, went AWOL frequently, and as a result spent several short terms in the guardhouse.

He did, however, fight bravely during an engagement at Murfreesboro, Tennessee, on July 13, 1861. But Col. Nathan Bedford Forrest's cavalry captured the entire Union garrison there. En route to a Confederate prison, the little drummer escaped. Three weeks later, the homesick youth applied for a discharge and was sent back to Detroit.

After visiting his mother briefly, on August 19 he re-enlisted in the 8th Michigan Infantry. Two days after his adventures in Fredericksburg, Hendershot was slightly wounded in the leg. News of his exploits had found its way to Horace Greeley, editor of the *New York Tribune*. Sensing a good story, he wrote Burnside that if the general would send Hendershot to him he would "present the boy with as fine a drum as could be made."

Burnside consented and that was the end of Hendershot's active service. Newspapers across the country lionized the "drummer boy of the Rappahannock." He went on the lecture circuit making patriotic appeals, P.T. Barnum hired him for awhile and he made a tour of England in 1863.

Following the war, President Grant appointed him postal clerk on the Lake Shore and Michigan Southern Railroad, a job he kept for 18 years. He then returned to the limelight, traveling around the country to veterans' reunions playing the fancy drum Greeley had given him. By 1903 his son, J.C., had joined him in the act, playing a gold-plated fife.

Shortly after the Civil War, a survey identified 127 Union volunteers who had enlisted at the age of 13 or younger. There were undoubtedly many others who had lied about their age. But none was more colorful than Michigan's "drummer boy of the Rappahannock."

In 1903, Hendershot posed with drums and son, J.C. Hendershot.

Beavers, Michigan's First Economic Base

An old beaver hunter poses beside a stump gnawed by beavers during varying levels of snow cover.

Lewis Henry Morgan crouched on a scaffold high in a tree one summer night in 1864. The full northern moon bathed the scene before him in a silvery light. He could plainly see the big beaver dam and the placid pond behind it, ringed with the jagged white stumps of beaver-gnawed trees. All was still save the gurgle of water through the breach in the dam Morgan had made in hopes of luring the elusive rodents out to repair their engineering marvel.

It was about 1 a.m. when Morgan spied the vee of ripples made by the dark heads of two swimming beavers. They cautiously approached the dam, clambered up its side and began to survey the damage that had caused the water level at their lodges upstream to fall.

Suddenly, one of the beavers spotted Morgan and dove into the pond. His great tail slapped the water with a loud crack. Before the last of the white spray had fallen back into the water, both beavers had disappeared. Realizing his beaver-watching was over for that night, Morgan made his way north approximately two miles to the frontier mining town of Ishpeming.

Morgan, remembered today as one of the fathers of modern American anthropology, had first come to the Marquette area in 1855 to survey the progress of the Iron Mountain Railroad, of which he was a director. As the railroad progressed west from Marquette and south of Teal Lake it intersected "a beaver district, more remarkable, perhaps, than any other of equal extent to be found in any part of North America."

For the next 12 summers Morgan returned to the iron country to study beavers. He collected their skulls and logs they had gnawed, photographed their dams and lodges, carefully mapped out the extent of their territory, interviewed local trappers and Indian guides, and in the process became an expert on the fabled creatures. He published an extensive monograph in 1868, *The*

American Beaver and His Works, that remains a classic in the field.

It was fitting that the first scientific study of North America's largest rodents, sometimes weighing 60 pounds or more, should be based on Michigan observations. Centuries before the thud of the lumberjack's ax startled the wilderness, before the pioneer hawed and geed his ox team, before the railroad builders and the copper miners, Michigan's economy rested firmly on beaver pelts. Traders and trappers in search of beaver first explored much of the peninsulas.

Beaver originally had been hunted not for their pelts, but for their perineal glands, which contained a desirable musky secretion. Known as castoreum, or castors, those dried glands were widely used in early medicine. Hippocrates, in fact, mentioned the medical value of castoreum as early as 500 B.C.

A treatise on the medical-chemical uses of beaver appeared in 1685. According to it, castoreum had become a panacea good for everything from headaches to hiccups. Other parts of the beaver, including the teeth, blood, skin and fat, were thought to have additional curative powers.

Beaver, once common throughout Europe, were so sought by apothecaries, that they became scarce except in Russia. The discovery in the 16th century that beaver fur made excellent felt, and in particular European fashion preferences for beaver hats, spurred a frenzied rush for North American beaver pelts.

Originally an estimated 100 million beaver ranged over most of the North American continent. The beaver figures prominently in Indian mythology. The creation myths of the Algonquin tribes, for example, feature a giant beaver that dove down to bring up the mud with which the Great Manitou fashioned the earth. Indians also hunted beaver as a food source - the tail, in particular, was considered a delicacy - fashioned chisels from their teeth and utilized beaver pelts for winter clothing. But when white traders offered knives, hatchets, firearms and firewater for beaver pelts the great slaughter was on.

The fur trade loomed large in the economy of the various new world colonies and beaver pelts became the standard by which everything else was valued. In 1623, the Dutch at New Netherlands adopted the beaver as the first public seal. The English, who took over New Netherlands in 1664, renaming it New York, developed the fur trade to an even greater extent. But the French, who controlled Canada and the interior of the American continent, enjoyed the greatest success.

Michigan's many streams and lakes rendered it prime beaver country. The French established their fur-trading headquarters for the Great Lakes at Sault Ste. Marie during the 17th century. Shortly thereafter it shifted to strategically located Michilimackinac. Cadillac removed the trading headquarters to Detroit, which he founded in 1701. But as the beaver and other fur-bearing animals grew scarcer in lower Michigan, Mackinac Island again became the hub of a gigantic fur-trading network that extended to the Mississippi River Valley.

Ultimately, French and British rivalry over the lucrative fur trade brought about the French and Indian Wars, which resulted in British possession of Michigan. Following the Revolutionary War, the British surrendered Detroit and Mackinac Island to the Americans in 1796. But British traders remained dominant until after the War of 1812. At that point, John Jacob Astor established his American Fur Company with headquarters at Mackinac Island.

The French and British had been careful to conserve their sources of supply. A regulation of the Hudson's Bay Company, for example, provided for a five-year interval between trapping seasons in particular beaver districts. However, the Americans, with true Yankee zeal, pursued the beaver without thought of conservation. Astor made a fortune from furs, but by the late 1820s, as beavers became increasingly scarce, Mackinac Island's economy shifted from fur to fish.

For some reason the trappers had apparently overlooked the large concentration of beavers discovered by Morgan in the iron country. Morgan mapped out 63 beaver dams varying from 50 to 500 feet in length. The ponds they created covered areas of up to 60 acres.

His intensive research also dispelled some of the many folk beliefs concerning the animals. They do not, for example, use their tails to carry mud for mortar, or to slap the mud into place in the crevices of the dams. Neither are they able to fell trees in a desired direction. Many of the trees of up to 18 inches in diameter dropped by beavers fall not in the water, but in whatever direction they are leaning.

Nevertheless, the remarkable construction abilities of beavers, which have for centuries altered the landscape, continue to make them one of nature's most fascinating creatures. No animal has had a greater impact on the historical development of Michigan.

James Redpath Originates Memorial Day

Artist L.D. McMorris' rendition of the first Memorial Day ceremony.

Schoolchildren, dressed in their Sunday best and carrying bouquets of wild flowers, led the procession. Then came a group of black clergymen, followed by a marching company of bluecoated soldiers. Singing patriotic hymns, the children circled the old race course at Charleston, South Carolina that had been converted into a cemetery for Union soldiers. Local dignitaries made stirring speeches, everybody saluted the Stars and Stripes and the children laid their bouquets before the simple wooden crosses.

This first formal Memorial Day celebration took place on May 1, 1865. James Redpath, who originated the idea, had emigrated at the age of 17 with his family from Scotland to Martin Township, Allegan County, in 1850. Redpath had studied the printing trade in Scotland and the backbreaking labor of subduing the wilderness held little appeal. After a few months he turned his back on the ax and plow forever and hiked 20 miles to the nearest printing office in Kalamazoo.

George A. Fitch, editor of the *Michigan Telegraph*, was away on a business trip to Detroit, so Redpath camped on the doorstep of the newspaper office until Fitch returned two days later. When the editor arrived at his office at daybreak, the eager young Scot was waiting for him. Fitch told him he needed no extra help, but he took Redpath to breakfast, during which the youth so impressed him that he relented. Decades later, Redpath remembered Fitch's words: "Well, if you can write as well as you can talk, perhaps I might find something for you to do." Redpath could not only write, as he soon demonstrated, but he could set up a story in type without even using a manuscript.

Ambitious and determined to find a wider audience for the fiery abolitionist editorials he was producing, Redpath stayed only a few months in Kalamazoo before going to Detroit. There he secured a job with another newspaper. A year later his editorials so impressed the leading journalist of the time, Horace Greeley of the *New York Tribune*, that Greeley wrote Redpath to come east, young man. He did, and by the time he was 19 Redpath had become an editor on the *Tribune*.

Beginning in 1854, Redpath traveled throughout the south interviewing slaves and slave owners and publishing their stories under the title of the "roving editor." He went to Kansas as special correspondent for the *St. Louis Democrat* and reported on the bloody atrocities committed there. However, Redpath championed John Brown's insurrection and later wrote a biography of Brown that helped mold him into the heroic figure he little deserved. Following two trips to Haiti in 1859, Redpath founded a Haiti Immigration Bureau, which promoted black expatriation to that country.

During the Civil War, Redpath followed the armies of Gen. William T. Sherman and Gen. George H. Thomas as a war correspondent and in 1863 he reported on Gen. Quincy Adams Gillmore's siege of Charleston. The city held out, however, until February 1865 when the Confederate forces evacuated it.

Redpath was appointed Superintendent of Education at Charleston and he also founded the Colored Orphan Asylum there. While visiting an old race course that had been converted into a Union cemetery, Redpath was so appalled at finding cattle grazing among the sunken graves that he formed a society made up largely of freed slaves to fence and maintain the grounds. The blacks agreed to dedicate one day a year to decorate the graves with flowers and on May 1, 1865, the first Decoration Day ceremony took place.

The idea gradually caught on in other cities across the country. In 1868, Gen. John A. Logan, commander of the Grand Army of the Republic, a Union veteran organization, issued a general order for all GAR posts to designate May 30th "for the purpose of strewing with flowers or otherwise decorating the graves of comrades who died in defense of their country during the late rebellion." May 30th was chosen because flowers would be in full bloom in even the northernmost states.

In 1873, New York became the first state to declare Decoration Day a legal holiday and gradually all of the other northern states did likewise. In the 20th century, as the ranks of the Civil War veterans grew thinner, those who died in America's other wars also came to be honored on May 30. As early as 1882, the GAR campaigned to designate the holiday as Memorial Day. But Decoration Day continued in popular usage due in part to verses written by Michigan's poet laureate, Will Carleton, that were traditionally read at graveside observances. Carleton included "Cover Them Over" in his *Farm Legends* published in 1875.

Cover them over with beautiful flowers,
Deck them with garlands, those brothers of ours,
Lying so silent by night and by day,
Sleeping the years of their manhood away.
Give them the meed they have won in the past;
Give them the honors their future forecast;
Give them the chaplets they won in the strife;
Give them the laurels they lost with their life.

Following the war, Redpath went on to greater glories. In 1868, he founded the Redpath Lyceum Bureau, which for decades brought leading speakers, including Ralph Waldo Emerson, Julia Ward Howe, P.T. Barnum, Josh Billings and Mark Twain, to rostrums across the nation. In the twentieth century, Redpath's firm merged with the Chautauqua movement and the Redpath Chautauqua Circuit staged week-long Chautauqua extravaganzas that first brought culture to hundreds of rural midwestern communities.

Redpath was run over by a New York City hack in 1891 and he died as a result of his injuries. Strangely enough, on his deathbed the man who had invented Memorial Day requested a very simple funeral with no flowers.

Unwilling Michigan Cavalrymen Help Win the West

Sioux warriors torturing to death Michigan cavalrymen in 1865.

The hot August sun beat down on the 11 cavalrymen and one civilian stagecoach driver who huddled behind the wagons they had fashioned into a fort. They were somewhere between the Big and Little Laramie rivers in southern Wyoming. Seventeen-year-old Alfred S. Livermore of the 7th Michigan Cavalry could feel the Sioux war arrows thudding into the stack of hardtack boxes that served as his shield. A bead of sweat trickled down his face.

The youth had left his home in East Saginaw seven months before to fight Johnny Rebs. Now, on August 4, 1865, nearly four months after the Confederate surrender at Appomattox, here he was pinned down by hundreds of hostile Indians in the middle of a Godforsaken no man's land. The chances of his making it back to Michigan, with his hair, looked mighty slim.

The unit Livermore had enlisted in at Flint on February 13, 1865, had won a reputation as one of the toughest in the entire Union cavalry. It was part of the famous Michigan Cavalry Brigade made up of the 1st, 5th, 6th and 7th Michigan Cavalry Regiments commanded by flamboyant Gen. George A. Custer. The brigade fought ferociously at Gettysburg and at 54 other engagements, principally in Virginia. Few other brigades enjoyed such esprit de corps and no other Union cavalry brigade suffered so high a percentage of men killed - 524 troopers.

Following Lee's surrender, the brigade was ordered to Washington D.C. to participate in a grand review on May 23, 1865. While in camp prior to the gigantic parade, Michigan Governor Henry Crapo had delivered an oration to the brigade, congratulating them on their brilliant record and remarking that "in a few more days they would be with friends and loved ones." Instead, shortly after the review, the Army ordered the brigade to Fort Leavenworth, Kansas.

The Michigan boys thought they had enlisted for three

years or for the duration of the war. On receiving the news that they were to be shipped west to fight Indians, "not one in fifty but acted like a wild man." Some 1,400 troops traveled via the Ohio, Mississippi and Missouri rivers to Fort Leavenworth. The only rations issued during the 14-day journey were hardtack (a big cracker so hard that it could break teeth) and raw bacon.

Seeking to discourage their officers from continuing the mission, the troops supplemented their limited fare by raiding the various river towns along the way. At Cincinnati the entire police force lined up to repulse the "Bloody Michigan Brigade." Nevertheless, squads of un-ruly cavalrymen marched through the city looting every saloon they discovered. Some returned to the boats carrying boxes of cigars and bottles of wine. Others rolled kegs of beer down the streets.

At Louisville a company of artillery had been stationed on a hill fronting the boat landing. With a wild yell and drawn sabers the Michigan veterans charged the position. The cannoneers retreated and the artillery wound up upside down at the bottom of the hill.

When the mutinous Michigan troops finally reached Fort Leavenworth, they were issued horses for the long trek to Denver. Hardtack, so hard it had to be pounded between stones before it could be eaten, and raw bacon were again the only rations. Ill-equipped for life on the plains and with insufficient water, the troops endured 34 days of hardship during their march to Denver. Of the original 1,400 soldiers who had left Washington, ap-proximately 750 deserted or died along the way.

Some of the troopers, with less than one year re-maining in their enlistment, were discharged shortly after their arrival. Despite repeated protests by Governor Crapo, the remainder were stationed at various outposts along the Bozeman Trail and other overland routes to protect stagecoaches and immigrant wagon trains from the Sioux, Cheyenne and Arapahoes who had gone on the warpath.

The Sixth Michigan Cavalry participated in the Powder River Expedition commanded by Gen. Patrick E. Connor. A detachment of Michigan men constructed and garrisoned Fort Connor, later renamed Fort Reno. Located on a bluff overlooking the Powder River, it was the first of a string of forts that guarded the Bozeman Trail.

While on that campaign, Capt. Osmer F. Cole of Galesburg strayed too far from the column. His troopers later found his body prickly with arrows.

A large war party of Arapahoes attacked another detachment of the Sixth Michigan Cavalry that was guarding a wagon train heading for Virginia City, Montana. The Indians "corraled" the train for 12 days until two Michigan men made a daring, 50-mile dash for reinforcements.

Not so lucky was another squad of Michigan cavalrymen on similar duty. The Sioux captured and tortured them to death on the Laramie Plains. Later, another company of soldiers wiped out the band of Sioux who had committed the atrocity. They discovered in their possession documents on which the Indians had recorded in pictographs the burning alive of the Michigan men while tied to wagon wheels.

Livermore and his companions knew a similar fate awaited them if they were captured. At dusk they mounted their horses and made a break for it, firing their revolvers as fast as they could. They had gone about a half-mile when they realized a teamster, Private George Baker from Jackson, had been left behind. They later learned that he was tortured and burned to death.

Mounted on their fast ponies, the Sioux pursued the Michigan cavalrymen. Periodically, the troopers dismounted to pepper the Indians with bullets and thus kept them at a distance. But they ran out of ammunition at the summit of a steep hill within a mile of safety. The

138

Indians caught up with them, killing three men and wounding three others. Young Livermore escaped, however, to fight again and to record his adventures in a book published in Saginaw in 1890.

Livermore and some other Michigan cavalrymen were finally relieved of duty in late November 1865. But the army would provide no transportation for them to travel the 1,400 miles back to Fort Leavenworth. They chartered a mule-drawn wagon train with their own money and arrived in Fort Leavenworth, where they were discharged on December 15. The rest of the soldiers from Michigan were consolidated into the First Michigan Veteran Cavalry and finally mustered out of service in Utah Territory on March 10, 1866.

Livermore returned to East Saginaw to work as a carpenter. He later operated a general store on Potter Street. In 1886, he launched a colorful career as a "temperance advocate and tobacco agitator," thrilling audiences across the state with stories of the evils of tobacco use as well as his own exploits fighting Indians out west.

The Great St. Louis
Magnetic Water Boom

In 1872, the Magnetic Water Bath House in St. Louis, Michigan, was 180 feet long.

The wood chisel flipped through the air, splashed into the stream of water that flowed from the artesian well and clanked against the iron well pipe. When the carpenter retrieved his tool he found it held fast to the pipe by a magnetic force. Soon the little Gratiot County lumber town of St. Louis buzzed with excitement over the mysterious phenomenon. Hundreds of area residents magnetized their pocket knives by stroking them against the pipe. Some swore their metallic objects turned magnetic merely by lying in the flowing water.

Then a crippled-up old drummer, as traveling salesmen were known, began drinking the water and immersing his rheumatic wrists and hands in the stream. It cured him completely! When news of his amazing recovery spread throughout the state, hundreds of invalids, pronounced incurable by physicians, flocked to St. Louis. They packed local hotels and overflowed into residences hastily converted into boarding houses. Before long the measured tapping of canes along the village's wooden sidewalks vied with the rap of carpenters' hammers busily nailing together additional hotels to accommodate the throngs of health seekers. The great St. Louis magnetic water boom was on.

Operators of the Holcomb and Evans sawmill had sunk the wonderful well during the summer of 1869. They hoped to strike a salt well similar to what had produced a thriving industry at Saginaw, 30 miles to the east. When they pounded a 3½-inch pipe 200 feet deep, a stream of water shot 28 feet into the air. But the gusher contained no salt.

Folks, in fact, found the clear sparkling water so delicious they began using it for household purposes. The town council debated buying the site as a municipal well and other entrepreneurs proposed laying a pipeline to Saginaw. But nothing came of these schemes until the accidental discovery of the water's curative powers a few months later.

In September 1869, Dr. Samuel P. Duffield, a professor of chemistry at the Detroit Medical College, analyzed a sample from the St. Louis well. He determined it contained "remedial agents equal to or superior in quantity and value to any mineral water in the world." He also called attention "to the fact of the current of electricity or magnetism that the stream of water carries."

Michigan's medical community parted company over the "magnetic water," however. Some thought the water had become magnetic by passing over giant lodestones buried deep within "the bowels of the state." Others explained the phenomenon as "terrestrial magnatism" caused by placing a long pipe in a line approaching the earth's magnetic dip. Some scientists said the water magnetized the pipe, others the pipe magnetized the water and still others that only the pipe was magnetic. Magnetism aside, most thought the mineral water beneficial for some medical ailments.

Belief in the remedial powers of mineral water had been part of American culture since colonial times. The Puritans had learned of mineral springs from the local Indians. Many were highly charged with sulphur and in tune with their Calvinist tenets the colonists thought the worse smelling and tasting the water the better it was for you. By the mid 1700s several fashionable spas had been established at East Coast mineral springs.

Dr. Benjamin Rush, a renowned medical authority of the late 18th century, conducted a survey of Pennsylvania's therapeutic springs. He was later much embarrassed to find that a Philadelphia well that was extremely popular because of its horrible-tasting water actually owed that property to drainage from a nearby privy.

Fortunately, Michigan's mineral springs proved more

hygienic. By the early 1870s thousands annually flocked to St. Louis. Civil War generals Dan Sickles and "Fighting Joe" Hooker found the magnetic water salubrious, as did Supreme Court Chief Justice Salmon P. Chase and famed detective Allan Pinkerton.

Following St. Louis' success, other enterprising Michiganders jumped on the water wagon. By 1870 some 60 wells, each claiming to be magnetic, had been bored throughout the state. Two years later, Dr. Stiles Kennedy, who had accepted the position of resident physician at the St. Louis Springs, published a book describing mineral and magnetic water industries at Alpena, Midland, Muskegon, Spring Lake, Fruitport, Three Rivers, Port Huron, Hubbardston, Menominee, Lansing, Albion, Grand Rapids, Owosso, Otsego, Grand Ledge, Eaton Rapids, Leslie and Rexford. Needless to say, the supply of springs soon proved "greatly in excess of the demand."

Some less-than-scrupulous proprietors hired "runners" to ride trains in an effort to con invalids into visiting their respective institutions. Kennedy cited the case of a lady traveling through Michigan with her invalid husband, "affected with softening of the brain." Three times she was befriended by "kind spoken gentlemen" who gulled her into journeying out of her way to visit various mineral water spas to no avail.

At the little community of Cascade, located on the Thornapple River just east of Grand Rapids, proprietors discovered mineral springs reputedly able to cure St. Vitus dance. They erected an elegant three-story hotel over the springs and enjoyed a thriving business until the springs undermined the foundations of the structure and it came crashing down.

Michigan's most successful mineral-bath industry began at Mount Clemens in 1873. The opulent Original, Media and Park bathhouses provided mineral baths for hundreds of thousands of Americans including William

Randolph Hearst, Henry Ford and Mae West. At the height of its prosperity in the 1920s, Mount Clemens boasted 10 bathhouses and more than 40 hotels.

But the Great Depression, more sophisticated medical theories and other factors brought an end to Mount Clemens' bathhouse era. The last surviving remnant of what had made the city one of the country's most famous spas, the Arethusa bathhouse, burned in 1976.

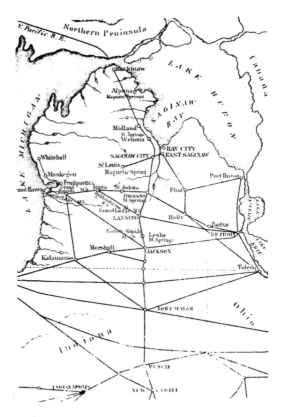

Michigan's magnetic and mineral spring sites in 1872.

Will Carleton, Michigan's Poet Laureate

"Over the hill to the Poorhouse, I'm trudgin' my weary way."

R. McCune, assistant editor of the *Toledo Daily Blade*, sat at his desk one morning in 1871 wearily examining the day's pile of unsolicited verse sent in by would-be poets. Rubbing the back of his aching neck, he began scanning a poem by Will M. Carleton of Hillsdale, Michigan. He shook his head, groaned a little and deftly flipped the sheet into the office's commodious wastebasket.

Later that morning, David Ross Locke, editor of the *Blade*, began rummaging in the wastebasket for a letter he had prematurely filed there. Finding Carleton's poem, he read the first verse:

> Draw up the papers, lawyer, and make 'em good and stout;
> For things at home are crossways and Betsey and I are out.
> We, who have worked together so long as man and wife,
> Must pull in single harness for the rest of our nat'ral life.

"What's this?" Locke asked his assistant. "Oh, some fellow who thinks he can write poetry, but can't even spell." Locke walked off, engrossed in the poem. Written in the vernacular of Michigan farm folks, the ballad told the touching tale of an old farmer who had decided to divorce his wife of many years. Yet he still cared enough for her to want to give her half of everything they had accrued during their marriage, an unnatural and unnecessary act according to 19th century legal practices.

Locke printed "Betsey and I Are Out" in the March 17, 1871, issue of the *Blade*. Within months it had been copied into nearly every newspaper in America. Thus was launched the national reputation of Michigan's "poet laureate," Will Carleton.

Born on October 21, 1845, in a farmhouse located two miles east of the Lenawee County village of Hudson,

William McKendree Carleton grew up in the rural life style he would later immortalize in verse. Frail and sickly as a child, he became a sensitive, dreamy youth, an omniverous reader who delighted in delivering mock orations.

Carleton's father, a stern New Englander, thought such activities were "spoiling a tolerably good farmer." Once when asked where his son was he replied, "Oh Will is probably in some apple tree writing an oration to deliver to the horses this evening." By the time he was 13, Carleton had begun writing poetry. One of his earliest surviving poems is a dirge for "The Dying Indian Chief."

Following graduation from a nearby one-room country school in 1861, Carleton began walking five miles a day to attend a graded school west of Hudson. But because his father insisted he work on the farm when needed, his attendance was irregular. Nevertheless, by 1862 he had learned enough to secure a position as a country-school teacher at a rate of $18 per month. That fall, Carleton also began attending Hillsdale College part time.

In addition to teaching, he financed his education by writing verse, newspaper articles and music and by reading his ballads before local audiences. Elected class poet, Carleton delivered a poem at his graduation exercises in 1869 that so moved the college president that he grabbed a bouquet of flowers and threw it at the poet as he descended from the platform.

Following graduation, Carleton went into full-time newspaper work, first with the Chicago-based *Western Rural* and then as editor of the *Hillsdale Standard.* While covering a divorce suit in the local circuit court in early March 1871, Carleton got the idea for "Betsey and I Are Out." He returned home and dashed off the poem that won him national acclaim.

His first collection of verse had been rejected by Scribner's, Harper's and several other publishers. Carleton had been forced to pay to have a small edition of his *Poems* published in Chicago. But as a result of the sensation created by "Betsey and I Are Out," Harper's and other publishers began clamoring for more of his ballads. He accommodated them with a series of sentimental poems depicting life in rural Michigan, including "Out of the Old House Nancy," "Gone with a Handsomer Man" and a happy sequel to his first popular poem "How Betsey and I Made Up."

During the summer of 1871, *Harper's Weekly* began publishing Carleton's ballads illustrated with appropriate woodcuts. On June 17, 1871, it first printed the poem destined to become Carleton's best known ballad, "Over the Hill to the Poor-House:"

"Over the hill to the poor-house I'm trudgin' my weary way --
I, a woman of seventy, and only a trifle gray --
I, who am smart an' chipper, for all the years I've told,
As many another woman that's only half as old.

Carleton thus related the sad story of a woman pushed out of her home by a daughter-in-law. As none of her other children would take her in, the only option left was the Hillsdale County Poorhouse. Carleton later mercifully saved the old lady in a sequel, "Over the Hill From the Poor-House."

Carleton's heart-throbbing verses, testifying that the shunting of the elderly out of sight and out of mind was practiced even in the "good old days," had a profound effect on thousands of readers. In the introduction to a special edition of the poorhouse poems issued 33 years later, Carleton acknowledged receiving many letters from superintendents of poorhouses reporting "a decrease in the number of inmates, occasioned by the withdrawal of old people, whose children were ashamed of their neglect."

In 1873 Harper's produced a beautifully illustrated edition of Carleton's *Farm Ballads*. It and the five other collections that appeared in a similar format over the succeeding two decades became best sellers, gracing the parlor tables of Victorian homes from coast to coast.

Carleton left Michigan for Boston in 1878. Four years later he married and moved to Brooklyn, N.Y., where he lived the remainder of his life. He edited a popular journal called *Every Where*, traveled the country as a well-paid stage lecturer, and continued to write poetry based on his Michigan experiences.

Carleton died in 1912. Eleven years later the Michigan legislature designated his birthday as a special holiday to be celebrated in all the state's schools. For many years, students in hundreds of one-room schoolhouses and sprawling urban high schools spent a portion of each October 21 studying Carleton's life and reciting his poetry.

Of Mice and Con Men

Austin (standing) and George Bidwell, bank robbers.

George Bidwell loved that little mouse like a brother - maybe better. It had been ten years since he had seen his real brother, Austin, who was serving out a life sentence in Chatham Prison near London, England. George, on the other hand, shared his narrow cell and prison fare with a pet mouse in the Woking lockup. The Bidwell brothers, former Grand Rapids and Muskegon residents, had earned their incarceration by pulling a $5 million forgery on the Bank of England in 1873, the first time that venerable institution had been so bilked.

Life in British "gaol" at that time was not exactly "a cup of tea." During his first six months of solitary confinement, George had been ill-used by a set of too-tight leg irons that rendered him a permanent cripple. But the cruel treatment, filthy little cell and abominable food were nothing compared to the lack of companionship. George saved his sanity by befriending any living creature that entered his cell. He had a succession of pet rats, flies and beetles. He even let mosquitoes drink their fill on his face just to hear the merry humming as they flew away. But of all his animal friends, he loved his mouse the most.

He spent endless hours teaching the little rodent tricks. His favorite was the dead-dog trick. The mouse would roll onto its back, legs up in the air, and play dead. When Bidwell commanded "Come to Life!" the mouse sprung up and ran along his arm into the safety of his breast pocket.

Despite the fact that the cell blocks swarmed with rats, mice and other vermin, strict prison rules prohibited pets of any kind. But Bidwell thought that if he showed the authorities how smart his mouse was they would make an exception. By then, he should have known "rules are rules."

Following an endearing demonstration of the dead-dog trick, Bidwell's "warder" grabbed the mouse and stomped him under his heel. Bidwell was "not afraid to

151

confess that I cried over the loss of this poor little victim of over confidence in human beings."

He described that and other prison horrors in an auto-biography, *Forging His Chains*, published in 1888. Brother Austin told his story in *From Wall Street to Newgate* published seven years later. The volumes detail how two Michigan boys followed the primrose path to penal servitude.

Born in Bloomfield, New York in 1833, George moved with his family four years later to Lanesville, later renamed Hudson, in Lenawee County. His parents were stern Methodists. He remembered how as a four-year-old he had been carried out of church and spanked by his father for falling asleep during a sermon. He and his siblings were not allowed to play games or listen to violin music and dancing was considered "an almost unpardonable sin." Indeed, the elder Bidwells regarded "everything in the way of amusement as time lost in making preparations for eternity."

Bidwell's father, in fact, spent so much time thinking about the hereafter that he allowed his earthly affairs to slip. He failed at several enterprises as the family moved from Hudson to Adrian, where Austin was born in 1845, then to Toledo.

Fortune finally smiled on the Bidwells in 1849 when they relocated to Grand Rapids and opened that community's first candy shop. George, who had developed business savvy through youthful hawking of lemonade and apples, was allowed to manage the operation. It prospered and the Bidwells moved from their original location on Monroe Street to a larger facility on Pearl Street and still later to Canal Street. In the meantime, George began sending out salesmen in wagons to supply surrounding dealers with wholesale candies.

But that increased overhead, in conjunction with the financial panic of 1855, proved disastrous. The Bidwell Candy Company went bankrupt due to the machinations of a shyster lawyer they had hired to help them liquidate assets. George sought a new life in New York City. The rest of the family moved to Muskegon.

The prospect of organizing a new Methodist Church had drawn the Bidwells to that rip-roaring lumber town. They found, however, more than they had bargained for as "whiskey selling, gambling, dog fighting and more brutal animal bipeds bruising each other, was the order of the day." The family tried to eke out an existence by operating a hotel. Unfortunately, most boarders were lumberjacks who, when asked by the elder Bidwell to pay, invited him out into the street to fight - winner take all.

Meanwhile, George, through dint of hard work, had launched a successful career as a wholesale grocery salesman. When he learned of his family's plight in Muskegon, he rented a house in South Brooklyn and sent for them. In 1857, his parents and seven siblings, including 12-year-old Austin, left Michigan for the Big Apple.

George married the following year and that made him the sole breadwinner for ten dependents. The pressure got to him, and he forged the first link of his chain by embezzling small sums from his employer. That chain rapidly lengthened through the assistance of bad companions. Brother Austin started on his path to perdition by petty gambling, then moved on to the big time - Wall Street.

By the 1870s the Bidwells had become hardened criminals specializing in forgery, bunco and assorted con games. Having made themselves personae non grata in much of the United States, they shifted operations to Europe.

A chance discovery that the prestigious Bank of England permitted reputable clients to draw cash against bills of exchange without investigating whether they were genuine, inspired the brothers and two confederates to pull the biggest caper of their career. They

153

set up an account and established credentials through a series of genuine bills of exchange. By January and February 1873 they were passing bogus bills for as much as $50,000 a day in gold.

They might have gotten away with the $5 million in gold they amassed within a few months' time had they not gotten greedy and careless. They accidentally left the date off one of their expertly forged bills. The clerk at the bank returned it to the supposed creditor to supply the omission and the forgery was discovered.

One of Bidwell's partners insisted on passing one final bill and got nabbed by the bobbies. George led the authorities a merry chase across England, Ireland and Scotland before they caught him. Austin was enjoying a nice dinner party in Havana, Cuba, when the long arm of the law, in the form of a Pinkerton detective, collared him.

Following a spectacular trial in England, all four forgers were sentenced to life imprisonment. George's wife and sister Harriet Bidwell Mott campaigned unrelentingly for his release. After serving 14½ years he was pardoned. Austin was finally released in 1891 and the other two partners the following year.

The Bidwell brothers took up residence in Hartford, Connecticut, where the two volumes of their confessions were published. Their sister Harriet lived until her death in 1909 at a farm on the south shore of Muskegon's Mona Lake, which the family had acquired in the 1860s.

Years after the Bidwell brothers had gone to their respective rewards, rumors surfaced that gold coins had been plowed up in the vicinity of the family farm. Before giving up in despair, treasure hunters had so pocked the fields near Mona Lake that one observer reported it looked like "the results of an earthquake."

Michigan Celebrates
the Centennial

The Michigan Building was erected at Philadelphia's Fairmount Park for the Centennial Exposition.

The steady rain that fell throughout the morning of July 4, 1876, had turned the streets of downtown Adrian into a muddy morass. Nevertheless, thousands of gaily dressed celebrants thronged the city. When the clouds showed signs of breaking up about 11 a.m. the big parade began.

Brass bands, militia regiments, veterans organizations, plumed Knights Templar commanderies, fire companies and other marching units swelled the mile-long procession. Hundreds of uniformed legs, plastered to the knees with mud, stepped in unison. Hundreds of feet squished ankle deep into the muck and lifted with a rhythmic sucking noise. But it would take more than a little rain to dampen the spirits of Michiganders who had assembled to honor the "spirit of 76" with the biggest and most colorful 4th of July ever.

America had begun planning its 100th birthday celebration on March 3, 1871, when a congressional act created a Centennial Commission composed of representatives of the various states. Michigan Governor Henry P. Baldwin appointed James Birney of Bay City as Commissioner, but when Birney was named minister to the Netherlands in 1875, Victory P. Collier of Battle Creek succeeded him. The Centennial Commission publicized and promoted the Centennial Exposition to be opened in Philadelphia's Fairmount Park on May 10, 1876.

Baldwin's successor, Governor John J. Bagley, stirred interest in the project, and the legislature passed an act on April 28, 1875, authorizing a board of managers representative of the state's "agricultural, pomological (fruit growing), mining and manufacturing interests" to supervise Michigan exhibits. Since only $7,500 was appropriated for expenses, free enterprise would have to fund Michigan's role.

Michigan lumbermen, then in the heyday of logging off the state's vast stands of timber, went all out to promote their industry. Lumber dealers from Detroit, Saginaw, Bay City, Muskegon, South Haven and Lapeer donated material to erect the Michigan Building. The 48-by-58 foot Gothic structure whose tower reached a height of 92 feet was finished inside and out with prize white pine, hardwoods and elaborate parquetry. Considered "the finest among all the state buildings," it served as an exhibit area and as a place of refuge for Michigan visitors to the fair. A gala grand opening held on July 6, featured a musical rendition of:

> Come along, come along
> Don't take alarm
> For Michigan is big enough
> To give us all a farm

The approximately 10 million visitors who wound their way through the five huge exhibition buildings that covered a total of 48 acres found many other choice Michigan products - 3,800 distinct specimens including 1,200 varieties of wood, 210 grasses, 540 samples of wool from 42 counties and 370 prehistoric artifacts. The state's horticulturists led the nation in the quantity and quality of fruit displays and, in particular, Michigan apples stole the show. Other popular exhibits were four masses of native copper weighing five tons each from the Central Mine in the Keweenaw Peninsula and a 15-ton chunk of iron ore from the Cleveland Mine near Marquette.

Those unable to attend the Centennial Exposition enjoyed plenty of excitement back home in Michigan. On February 22, 1876, Gov. Bagley issued a proclamation urging every citizen of the state on April 15 "to plant a tree, which our children and our children's children may know and remember as the tree planted by patriotic hands in the first centennial year of the Republic." Michigan, the only state to adopt that form of celebration, responded en masse to Bagley's suggestion.

Communities across the peninsulas staged elaborate ceremonies and in others schoolchildren or individuals quietly planted thousands of shade trees on public grounds or along roads.

The Ann Arbor Turn-Verein, a German club, marched to a park about half a mile southwest of the city where each member planted a tree. In Allegan, citizens cut down the old locust trees that lined city streets and planted 800 "vigorous young maples." Monroe residents placed fruit trees along the highways "so that the tired traveler might not only enjoy their grateful shade, but might find refreshment in their fruit." Holland's Dutch colonists transplanted a variety of trees in the newly platted Centennial Park.

Centennial excitement had reached a fever pitch by the 4th of July. Michigan communities greeted midnight of the third with New Year's Eve-type frivolity. All the church bells in Flint rang out at midnight as well as factory whistles, firecrackers and a 13-gun salute. Citizens lined Muskegon streets awaiting the midnight hour "to commence the ding-dong of jubilation which lasted for over an hour."

Rain in varying amounts doused Michigan communities the next morning. In Grand Rapids it merely laid the dust and freshened the air. Some 25,000 visitors joined residents there in marveling at a two-mile-long parade and the 84-foot-high Centennial Arch, decked with huge patriotic paintings, that had been erected on Campau Place.

The parade at Bay City featured horse-drawn floats. D.A. Root & Co's padlock factory, Albert Miller's copper shop and A.C. Braddock & Co's oar factory contributed floats on which company artisans plied their respective trades. The Eagle Brewery piled a wagon high with barrels of its popular beverage.

The entire city of Jackson was gaily decorated with hundreds of flags and banners. Following the parade and lunch, an "immense concourse of people" gathered on the public square for elocutionary exercises. The Rev. Moses Smith told of listening to stories about Revolutionary War battles on his veteran grandfather's knee. After the speeches came athletic events and a demonstration of the city's new water works.

In Kalamazoo, flags draped "every available space" on downtown business blocks, factories and homes. A great liberty bell fashioned from evergreen boughs with a tongue of tri-colored flowers hung over the speaker's stand at the courthouse. There Asa Stoddard, the farmer poet from Cooper, regaled the crowd with a long epic poem beginning:

> We hail with pride, as well we may,
> With joy and exultation
> This glorious and immortal day,
> Centennial of our nation.
> Let party strife be put away,
> Away with care and sadness;
> And let us give our hearts today
> To patriotic gladness.

In many communities, comically-costumed citizens staged early morning Mardi Gras-type parades, followed by an official parade later. Allegan had its "Klu Kluxes," Bronson its "Fantastics," Union City its "Horribles," and in Marquette the "Calithumpians" provided "a happy hit and lucky send-off." The official parade in Marquette featured a seven-ton block of sawed sandstone pulled by six horses.

Saginaw City and East Saginaw, then separate entities, joined in a grand celebration. An evergreen arch suspended between the courthouse and county buildings carried the appropriate motto "What from our father's heritage is lent, earn it yourself to really possess it." Like many other communities, the Saginaws held athletic events in the afternoon, a greased pole climb, and wheelbarrow, sack, velocipede, and firemen's races.

The greased pig itself was the prize for that event as was the fowl in the memorable "catching the rooster with hands tied contest."

As soon as "night had hung her curtain and pinned it with a star" most communities lit up the sky with elaborate fireworks displays, a fitting finale to the great centennial celebration of July 4, 1876.

Visitors thronged the huge Agricultural Hall at the Centennial Exposition.

The Man Who Hated to Walk

George Sheffield's 1887 model two-man railroad velocipede.

George S. Sheffield hated to walk. He figured he had done enough marching during his three-year stint in the 11th Michigan Infantry during the Civil War to last him the rest of his life. After the war he had settled down on a farm about 10 miles east of Three Rivers. There he spent another seven years plodding endless miles behind a horse-drawn plow.

Then he got a job as a mechanic with Jonathan Willits and Son, a Three Rivers pump manufacturer. Ten hours a day, six days a week he labored - that was the normal factory work week in the 1870s. Sheffield roomed in town during the week and went home on Saturday night for his one day off.

The problem was that the Michigan Central Railroad ran no passenger cars to the east after noon on Saturday or to the west before noon on Monday. Livery rental was too expensive for a working man. So the tired mechanic hiked along the railroad tracks on Saturday night and early Monday morning - nearly 10 miles each way. And Sheffield really hated to walk.

"Necessity is the mother of invention," and Sheffield had a need. He had plenty of time to mull over that need as he trudged along the tracks and he also had mechanical skills. So during the winter of 1877 he began tinkering on a gadget that he thought might satisfy his need. He called it a velocipede car after what early bicyclists called their machines. His contraption looked something like a bicycle on train wheels. A third wheel, attached like an outrigger, allowed it to fit the train tracks. But unlike a bicycle, the operator pumped the handlebars back and forth to power the rear wheel. Sheffield did not mind using his arms and back to get from one place to another - he just hating walking.

His first experimental model had some bugs in it, but by 1878 he had perfected his velocipede and he promptly patented it. At night and without authorization from the railroad company, Sheffield and his little invention merrily clacked along the tracks. But one winter night on his way home the velocipede was suddenly thrown off the tracks by a broken rail.

He had become familiar enough with the train schedule to know that a freight train was due shortly. There would be a wreck unless he could head it off. Sheffield ran to a nearby farmhouse, borrowed a lantern, flagged down the train and then helped the crew repair the track. Grateful Michigan Central officials later examined the velocipede and gave Sheffield permission to operate it over that stretch of track. They also asked him to build several more for the use of their track inspectors.

The velocipedes proved so successful that orders began pouring in from other railroads. In 1879, Sheffield formed a partnership with his former boss's son, Warren Willits, and went into production. They soon added a novel light handcar to their line and by the end of the year Sheffield velocipedes and handcars were in use by over 100 American and foreign railroads.

Other businesses also found the velocipede ideal when they could get permission to use them on the rail lines. A western Pennsylvania newspaper, the *Oil City Derrick*, purchased one to deliver papers to neighboring Franklin. In 1880, the editor, obviously a frustrated poet, penned:

What is it that each morning bright
   Takes down to Franklin great delight
To every Derrick reader?
   'Tis nothing else under the sun
Than that mysterious son-of-a-gun
   The Derrick's three-wheeled speeder.

Within a few years those mysterious son-of-a-guns were making inventor Sheffield a rich man. But for some unknown reason he sold his interest in the firm in 1883. Sheffield moved to Bronson in Branch County where he continued his tinkering. In 1891 he patented a novel type of hand corn planter. He set up a factory in the St. Joseph County village of Burr Oak for its manufacture. That venture also proved a success and by the turn of the century Sheffield was shipping his corn planters to "all civilized parts of the world." He became one of Burr Oak's "leading citizens," organized the First National Bank there and the South Michigan Telephone Company.

Meanwhile the company he had sired in Three Rivers also stayed on the right track. The Sheffield Velocipede Car Company branched into other railroad specialties including the Dodge standpipe, a water spout used by steam locomotives to take on water; and cattle guards, beds of sharp spikes that kept livestock off the tracks. The company reorganized in 1884 and Charles H. Morse of the famous Fairbanks Morse Scales Company bought in. Within a few years it absorbed the Sheffield Car Company completely.

In 1896 the company introduced a line of gasoline-powered inspection cars - one- and two-man cars similar to Sheffield's original velocipede and larger four-wheel models capable of transporting an entire eight-man section crew. Next came various cars adapted to narrow gauge mining railroads. There were small, four-wheel models pedaled by one miner into the shaft, larger handcars for mine crews and machinery, and ore dump cars.

By 1912 some 1,200 employees worked at the massive Sheffield Car Company factory sprawled over 40 acres on the south side of Three Rivers. One-third of the city's residents depended directly on the company for their livelihood. During World War I and World War II the company turned to production of military equipment.

When World War II ended in 1945, the Sheffield Company also began producing a line of automatic coal stokers that saved endless trips to the basement to throw in shovelfuls of coal. But railroad cars remained the

164

bread-and-butter product.

Other southwestern Michigan companies developed products similar to Sheffield's velocipedes. The Kalamazoo Railroad Velocipede and Car Company, which later evolved into the Kalamazoo Manufacturing Company, went into production in the early 1880s. Its line of handcars were sold to railroads world-wide. In Australia "Kalamazoo" became the slang term for small gasoline-powered rail cars. Still in use in remote parts of the world are slightly more sophisticated versions of the railroad velocipede invented by the man who hated to walk.

A telegraph-car from Sheffield's 1887 catalog.

165

Julia Moore, the Sweet Singer of Michigan

Julia Moore, the "Sweet Singer of Michigan," in 1902.

It was a raucous crowd that packed Powers' Opera House in Grand Rapids the evening of May 1, 1877. When the curtain went up, thunderous applause greeted the short, homely woman who advanced at a gait more accustomed to traversing plowed fields than a polished wooden stage. Only 29 years old, she had already lost most of her teeth, thus rendering her face somewhat "angular," as one reviewer observed. Nevertheless, her dark eyes gleamed and her fashionable, new, black silk dress glistened in the limelight.

Her calloused hands clutched a little paper-covered volume of verse. Then Julia A. Moore began to recite the tragic ballad of "Little Libbie:"

One morning in April, a short time ago,
    Libbie was active and gay;
Her Savior called her, she had to go,
    E're the close of that pleasant day.

A wild ovation startled the poet. When the audience settled down she continued:

While eating dinner, this dear little child
    Was choked on a piece of beef.
Doctors came, tried their skill a while,
    But none could give relief.

Pandemonium broke loose in the galleries. The crowd shouted and stamped its feet. Each time Moore delivered a particularly sad and pathetic verse she was drowned out with cheers. Interpreting those interruptions as compliments, she proceeded through her repertoire of some of the worst poetry ever composed.

She apparently was the only one in the auditorium that failed to catch the joke. The whole performance, including much advance publicity, was a burlesque, and she was the butt of the humor. Accompanied by a three-piece orchestra from Rockford that played off-key and in discord, she closed the recital by singing her lyrics, "The Beautiful Twenty-Second," a tribute to Washington's birthday. At its conclusion, several young men from the audience presented her with a fragrant bouquet of cabbage blossoms.

Born December 1, 1847, in a log cabin in Plainfield Township, Kent County, Julia A. Davis received little formal education. Nevertheless, as a teen-ager she began to compose verse about everyday happenings. As she explained in an autobiographical poem:

It was my heart's delight,
To compose on a sentimental subject
If it came in mind just right

Death, particularly that of children, was a common occurrence on the Michigan frontier, and she specialized in funeral odes.

At the age of 18, she married Fred Moore. They lived on a farm near her home for a short time, and then ran a store at Edgerton, a hamlet three miles north of Rockford. The centennial celebration of 1876 moved her to assemble her best pieces for publication by a Grand Rapids printer. Moore's *Sentimental Song Book* went through six editions in two years. "The Sweet Singer of Michigan," as she was soon dubbed, received national publicity when her Cleveland publisher sent review copies to various newspaper editors.

Humorists across the country lampooned her verse as well as the portrait that appeared in the volume. Bill Nye included a chapter on her work in his humorous collection *Bill Nye and Boomerang.* He suggested her poetic license be revoked. Mark Twain parodied her verse and wrote in 1897 that she had given him joy for 20 years. Hoosier poet Eugene Field found her book so entertaining that he offered $50 for a first edition. Other members of the literati found the sweet singer's technique so bad, her subjects so morbid and her naivete so disarming that they applauded her poems as gems of humor.

Except for an occasional ode in honor of the Grand Rapids Cricket Club, local politicians or temperance, most of Moore's poems dealt with death. Nye counted 21 killed and nine wounded in her slim volume. "Julia is worse than a gatling gun," he concluded.

No less than three separate pieces, for example, chronicle the tragic fate of the William House family. Poor six-year-old Hattie House, who dropped dead amid her playmates, was the first to go:

Those little girls will not forget

> The day little Hattie died,
>   For she was with them when she fell in a fit
>   While playing by their side.

Hattie's teen-aged sister, Lois, caught some dread disease and expired following a quick kiss by her boyfriend:

> She gasped for her breath once or twice more,
>   When lo! her spirit left her, and Lois is no more.

What was left of the once-numerous House family moved from Kent County to seek healthier surroundings, but alas:

> They once did live in Edgerton,
>   They once did live at Muskegon,
> From which they went to Chicago,
>   Which proved their fatal overthrow.

The dire consequences of life in the wicked city are best left to the imagination.

Eventually Moore realized she was being laughed at - not with - especially when newspaper reporters began showing up at her home. In an "Address to the Public" included in an 1878 edition of her poems she regretted "signing my name to that little book when a fictitious name would have done just as well." Grand Rapids pranksters staged a return engagement of the sweet singer on December 23, 1878, but she got the last laugh. At the close of her reading she looked out at her hecklers and announced, "You people paid 50 cents each to see a fool, but I got $50 to look at a house full of fools."

At that point, Moore's husband forbade her to publish any more poetry. The Moores moved to a small settlement three miles north of Manton in 1882 where they spent the remainder of their lives in relative peace. Julia bore 10 children, but only six lived to adulthood. After her husband died in 1914, she published one final book, a novel. She died in 1920.

The final stanzas of her poem, "To My Friends and Critics," might have made an apt eulogy for the Sweet Singer:

> Dear Friends, I write for money,
>   With a kind heart and hand,
> I wish to make no enemies

Throughout my native land.
Kind friends, now I close my rhymes
    and lay my pen aside,
Between me and my critics
    I leave you to decide.

CENTENNIAL, 1876.

———

THE

SENTIMENTAL

SONG BOOK.

———

BY JULIA A. MOORE.

———

GRAND RAPIDS, MICH
C. M. LOOMIS BOOK AND JOB PRINTS
1876.

Title page of Julia Moore's first book of verse.

The Sinking of the Alpena

The Alpena, a 175-foot side-wheeler weighing 653 tons.

The pipe organ boomed out the familiar strains of the "Wedding March," as pretty 18-year-old Lottie Davis slowly advanced down the aisle of the Presbyterian Church in White Pigeon. The Rev. Samuel Hart tied the knot that forever bound in marriage his son, the Rev. Farel Hart, and Lottie. It was a beautiful Indian summer afternoon on October 14, 1880, and a large crowd of well-wishers had gathered for the ceremony. Yet, despite the joyousness of the occasion, "an unaccounted for sadness seemed to possess each heart," an air of foreboding.

The happy couple left that afternoon for a short honeymoon excursion. They took the train to Grand Rapids and the following afternoon rode to Grand Haven. Hart had recently accepted a position with the David C. Cook Company, a Chicago-based publisher of Sunday School literature, and he needed to return to work. At Grand Haven, the Harts boarded the steamer Alpena for what they anticipated as a pleasant voyage over the moonlit lake to Chicago.

Built in 1866, the 175-foot-long side-wheeler weighing 653 tons, recently had been refurbished. Owned by the Goodrich Transit Company, the Alpena plied the St. Joseph, Grand Haven, Muskegon and Chicago route. At Muskegon and Grand Haven, Captain Nelson W. Napier had taken on passengers, variously estimated at from 35 to 80, and a cargo of eight boxcars of apples and two carloads of wood shavings used to stuff mattresses. The vessel carried a crew of 26.

October 15 had been a fine warm and sunny day. But mariners had noted a rapid drop in the barometer. The lighthouse keeper at Grand Haven had warned Capt. Napier that a big blow was on the way. But Napier had replied that he thought he would be nearly across the lake before it struck.

At approximately 8 p.m., the crew cast off the moor lines and the two great side paddles of the Alpena churned the water white as it headed out of Grand Haven harbor. The wind grew steadily stronger and shifted to southwesterly. By 9 p.m. the storm had reached gale force and within a few hours the temperature dropped from 65 degrees to below freezing and it began to snow.

At Muskegon, pedestrians clung to lampposts to keep from being blown away as billboards and lengths of wooden sidewalks sailed through the air and smokestacks and church steeples toppled. Enormous waves battered Lake Michigan beaches, undermining the roots of ancient trees and sending them crashing into the surf. The storm, rated as the worst then experienced in the history of Lake Michigan, continued unabated the following day. Some 90 vessels sank, suffered damage or were run aground. One lighthouse keeper reported that the waters of Lake Michigan were white for a week after the storm. He theorized that the force of the tremendous waves had ground limestone rocks into a fine powder that was held in suspension.

On the morning of the 16th, the Alpena had failed to reach Chicago. Several vessels reported seeing her struggling through the troughs of the giant waves. As late as 5 that afternoon she was seen off the coast of Racine, Wisconsin. Her cargo had shifted, she was listing badly and one paddle wheel had lifted out of the water. The wind drove her to the northwest and although her exact fate will never be known, she apparently foundered somewhere near the middle of the big lake. All aboard "sank amid the war of winds and wave, benumbered with the sleet and ice and wind - sank beneath the green waters of Lake Michigan."

Relatives and friends kept up their hopes, but on the 19th wreckage from the Alpena began to wash ashore. The beach near Holland was littered with debris. Fire buckets stenciled with the ship's name, a battered piano, life preservers, cabin doors and the bodies of six passengers were recovered. Thousands of apples bobbed in the Lake Michigan surf for weeks. Two weeks later, a 5-by-10 foot flag with the name Alpena in large letters was discovered near the entrance to the White Lake channel at Whitehall.

Beachcombers found pathetic messages hastily scrawled by the vessel's passengers and crew - insurance papers sealed in a bottle, the bottom of a grape basket bearing a statement that the Alpena was sinking and all aboard knew they would perish and a similar message scratched by Capt. Napier on a shingle. A college professor found a section of the cabin washed up on the Holland beach. Tucked behind a piece of molding was a water-soaked note that read: "This is terrible. The steamer is breaking up fast. I am aboard from Grand Haven to Chicago." The signature of the writer was undecipherable. The only thing positively known about the Alpena's final fate was that all aboard perished.

A coroner's jury convened at Grand Haven on January 2 declared that the Alpena had not been seaworthy, most of the crew were inexperienced and the life preservers and lifeboats were unserviceable. The Goodrich Transit Company was found liable for the disaster. That verdict so angered crusty old Capt. Albert E. Goodrich that he suspended service to Grand Haven and Muskegon during 1881.

Memorial services for Farel and Lottie Hart, whose bodies the lake never gave up, were held in his father's church in Adrian; in Lake View, Illinois, where they intended to settle; and in White Pigeon. So many thronged to the White Pigeon Presbyterian Church during funeral services on October 31 that many could not get within hearing distance of speakers. Six pastors from the village's churches delivered memorial sermons. A booklet containing the ill-fated couple's likenesses and their sad story was privately published in 1881. It contains the poem "The Lost Alpena" penned by A. Brownell Wood of Muskegon:

At morn the ship was seen to brave
The raging hell of wind and wave,
Then passes from our kin;
Save that a few loved forms of clay
Tell what their mute lips may not say-
A wreck strewn beach, amid whose spray
The weary watchers hold their way,
Of hope bereft - they only pray,
"O Lake, give back my dead."

Pretty Lottie Hart, who went down on the Alpena.

Buffalo Bones

A mountain of buffalo skulls at the Michigan Carbon Works in Detroit.
(Photo courtesy Burton Historical Collection, Detroit Public Library)

James H. Cook and two other cow hands were riding east on the old Bozeman Trail in northern Wyoming Territory on a hot afternoon in 1881. Born and raised in southern Michigan, Cook had drifted west as a teen-ager to become a cowboy, Indian scout and hunting guide. In Michigan the 24-year-old had learned to shoot straight and to follow the hunter's creed - kill only what you can use. He well knew what a game hog was.

But when a small herd of buffalo suddenly appeared from behind a rugged butte a hundred yards ahead, he spurred his horse in pursuit. Six quick shots rang out from his Spencer carbine. Before his "blood had cooled" so that he knew what he was doing, six of the big shaggy animals lay panting out their last dying gasps.

Cook had no use for the buffalo meat or hides. Admitting to his friends that he had "just performed one fool stunt," he rode ruefully from the killing field. He might have felt even sadder had he realized that he had just senselessly slaughtered some of the last of a dying breed. By 1883, the 60 to 75 million buffalo that thundered across the western prairies but twenty years before had been reduced to a few thousand scattered refugees.

The Great Plains tribes had subsisted largely on buffalo for centuries. Despite such wasteful hunting techniques as stampeding entire herds off cliffs, they had made little impact on the animal's prodigious numbers. It was the coming of the white man that spelled the buffalo's doom. Professional hunters such as Buffalo Bill Cody supplied fresh meat daily for the railroad construction crews that bridged the continent. European gentlemen traveled to the far west for the sheer sport of shooting buffalo. Other sportsmen enjoyed firing into the herds as they rode the trains.

Then, in 1871, a young Vermonter named John Mooar discovered that properly tanned buffalo hides made a superior type of leather, ideal for shoes, saddles,

177

harnesses, etc. Within months an army of hide hunters fanned across the western plains to supply train loads of reeking buffalo skins to eastern tanneries.

Their bloody task was made easier by an unfortunate trait of buffalo to stand stupidly chewing their cud as marksmen picked them off one by one with heavy long-range rifles. Some lucky hunters thus managed to kill a hundred or more buffalo within an hour or so. By 1873 buffalo hides had so glutted the market that the price of even prime bull hides had dropped dramatically. The value of a majestic animal, weighing one ton or more, had been reduced to $1. Still the slaughter continued, as wagons heaped high with hides lumbered away from stretches of rotting carcasses.

Some U.S. cavalry officers encouraged the massacre. Without buffalo to hunt, the fierce plains tribes could be starved into submission. Kansas, where Michigan Potawatomi and Ottawa had been herded in the 1840s, was soon denuded of buffalo. The herds that once darkened the southern plains were practically gone by 1879. Thousands of hide hunters migrated to the northern ranges. During the season of 1881-82 one Montana dealer alone shipped over 250,000 hides.

Suddenly, in 1883 it was all over. A few hundred buffalo had reached the sanctuary of Yellowstone National Park. Here and there a solitary bull ranged in some desolate canyon. Endless stretches of bleached bones marked the fate of the rest of the buffalo.

Arthur E. Towne, whose family homesteaded in South Dakota in the 1880s, eventually settled down in Allegan County's Otsego Township. He published a book there in 1941 describing how he and his siblings had gathered bushel baskets full of buffalo horns on their farm. They used them to form distinctive borders around garden plots.

But for many other western homesteaders, bones became the first cash crop. Buffalo bones shipped by rail to eastern manufacturers were worth as much as $22.50 per ton. The horns and hooves were converted to glue and the bones themselves were baked and ground into fertilizer and bone black, a substance widely used to filter and purify sugar.

The Michigan Carbon Works, founded in Detroit in 1873, eventually became one of the nation's largest consumers of buffalo bones. In 1880, the firm acquired a 73-acre tract on the River Rouge near the Detroit suburb of Delray. There company founders Deming Jarvis and William Hooper constructed a massive factory for converting western buffalo bones into glue, bone char, neat's-foot oil and fertilizer. Local citizens soon dubbed the company town that sprang up nearby "Boneville."

Three years later the firm had become "the most extensive and complete carbon works in the United States." By 1885 over 10,000 tons of bones, equivalent to the remains of approximately 200,000 buffalo, were being converted annually. In 1892, the Michigan Carbon Works sprawled over 100 acres, employed 750 workers and had become one of Detroit's largest industries.

But by the 1890s the handwriting was on the wall for the company's source of supply. The commerce in buffalo bones was rapidly going the same way as the buffalo themselves. The firm began stockpiling bones. One pile of bones on company property was 20 feet high, 20 feet wide and the length of a football field. Before the supply ran out in the mid 1890s the Michigan Carbon Works and other such plants in St. Louis and elsewhere had processed the bones from an estimated 40 million buffalo.

With the buffalo gone, the plains Indians were soon defeated and the great West was wide open for exploitation by cattle ranchers and farmers. In 1895, there were only 800 buffalo in all of North America. Miraculously the American bison was snatched from the brink of extinction by the efforts of a few conservationists. A census in 1972 located roughly 33,000 living specimens of the animal that has become symbolic of the freedom of the old west.

The buffaloes' last stand (1872).

19th Century Michigan Christmas - Bah Humbug!

This Victorian Santa Claus found an ample hearth.

It was late Christmas Eve, 1881. Dr. Washington A. Engle, physician, postmaster, merchant and self-styled poet, sat before the hearth's dying embers in his home in the Van Buren County village of Hartford. The rest of the family had retired for the night, but he wanted a little time alone to think over the busy day's events and to make peace with his diary. Besides, he sort of felt a poem coming on.

Engle opened his little diary, dipped pen in ink and scrawled in his crabbed handwriting: "Saturday December 24, 1881. Weather warm and pleasant all day. I am at store very busy selling goods for Christmas, $74.00 taken in." Not exactly a take calculated to brighten the heart of a modern-day merchant, but in an era when skilled factory workers earned roughly $1.25 for a ten-hour day, Engle had cause for celebration.

Perhaps that is why he had splurged on a gift for his wife that year. He recorded, "I put on Christmas tree a gold watch and chain for wife costing 58 dollars cash at nearly wholesale price." She had reciprocated in a considerably less generous manner. "I get a reclining chair from wife worth $9.00," Engle tersely noted. The entry in his diary for Christmas one year later revealed how he settled that score: "I pay for gloves for wife, $1.75."

Like Engle, many 19th century Michigan residents faithfully recorded their everyday activities in diaries. Hundreds of the little leather-bound volumes that have survived provide a peep at Christmas past. Ebenezer Scrooge, it appears, would have felt right at home in early Michigan.

Take Benjamin Farley, a pioneer preacher, for example. Modern-day remodelers found several years of his diaries secreted within the walls of the home he built west of Burr Oak in St. Joseph County. On December 25, 1837, he wrote "at home - hauled wood and regulated things." Christmas day four years later found him again "at home - not very well - pleasant weather." Not one of his diaries contains even a mention of Christmas.

The Puritans who settled New England long considered Christmas celebrations taboo. Christ's birthday was a time for religious introspection, not to be spent in frivolous festivities with a pagan origin. Seventeenth century New Englanders faced a stint in the stocks for publicly celebrating Christmas. Not until 1856 did Christmas become a legal holiday in Massachusetts. The bulk of the pioneers who streamed into Michigan during the 1820s and 1830s came from New England or were the children of New Englanders who had settled in western New York the generation before. They apparently brought to Michigan a similar aversion to Christmas cheer.

George DeLano, a pioneer farmer who settled in Cooper Township, Kalamazoo County, spent Christmas day in 1855 getting his "horses shod at Packards," following which he "mended the sled and loaded wood for Kalamazoo." Other Christmases in the 1850s found him paying his taxes, collecting mail at the post office and in general going about his business as if it were any other day of the year. The highlight of December 25, 1857, was his attendance at a temperance lecture. His first mention of the holiday occurred in 1865 when, after the usual round of chores, the family sat down to a "Christmas chicken pie."

Other contemporary diary entries indicate that stores, post offices, and factories routinely stayed open on Christmas Day. Women's diaries show little letup from the harsh routines of housework. If December 25 fell on a Monday it was washday, Christmas or not.

But the 1860s mark a turning point in the evolution of Christmas in Michigan. Perhaps Civil War veterans had seen how the holiday was celebrated in other parts of the country, particularly the South where it had long been a cherished festive occasion. Perhaps the arrival of immigrants from Germany, Holland and other European nations with traditions of Christmas trees and Santa Claus had helped popularize it. Or maybe it was the increased availability of nationally circulated magazines carrying Christmas stories and colorful advertisements. In any event, for whatever the reason, Christmas trees, celebrations and gift-giving appear with greater frequency in diaries beginning in the 1860s.

George Reynolds of Berrien Springs, then the county seat of Berrien County, consistently sawed wood on Christmas day from 1855 to 1862. But in 1863 he recorded, "was a Christmas tree over to the court house - distributed presents in the evening." That was how it began in many Michigan communities - one large Christmas tree in a courthouse, school, church or Grange Hall. Those who participated arranged their family's gifts on the tree and showed up on Christmas Eve or day for a communal celebration made brief due to the shortness of the candles that provided the solitary decorations.

In 1869, Sally Haner of Three Rivers recorded in her diary the sad story of her sister who had gone to a local schoolhouse to see the Christmas tree "but it was all over with when she got there" - the candles had burned out. By 1875 Reynolds mentioned two Christmas trees in Berrien Springs, at his church and the Grange Hall. Two years later he counted four communal trees.

Christmas gifts then were usually inexpensive and utilitarian in nature. Fourteen-year-old Frank Stuart of Schoolcraft Township in Kalamazoo County wrote in 1879, for example, "Christmas morning I got a lantern, Arthur a diary, Chas a knife, father a pocketbook, mother a scarf, Libbie a book and Lena a doll." Esther Lawrence of Volinia Township in Cass County was delighted Christmas morning 1875 when she "found a new clothes wringer in place of the old one," just in time for washday two days later.

Some diarists recorded the amount of money they spent at Christmas time. George C. Adams, a farmer from Comstock Township in Kalamazoo County, itemized his "cash out" for Christmas 1876: "2 quarts oysters 70 cents, hooks for pictures 5 cents, cord for picture frames 25 cents, plans for motto frames 20 cents, thimble for wife 50 cents." The children received framed mottos, his wife a thimble and they all enjoyed an oyster dinner, more common at that time than turkey or ham as a Christmas feast - total expenses $1.70.

Christmas celebrations have changed dramatically since the simpler days of the 19th century. But perhaps Dr. Engle of Hartford captured the true spirit of Christmas in the final lines of the poem he wrote that Christmas eve of 1881 while the rest of the household slept and the fireplace flickered:

"And while, this eve, good gifts we give, and share,
With inner feelings, tongue can not declare,
Let's not forget the gift that God has given,
His only son, to show the way to heaven."

Dr. John Harvey Kellogg
and the
Battle Creek Sanitarium

Dr. John Harvey Kellogg, proprietor of the Battle Creek Sanitarium, who invented peanut butter, cornflakes and granola for his patients.

The Rev. W.B. Hill clung to a set of iron rings protruding from the wall above his head while an attendant rubbed his naked body with handfuls of wet rock salt. The sharp crystals nearly cut through his skin. After the "salt glow," he got a shower that gradually became so cold he "could scarcely endure it." He felt better after the vigorous massage that followed.

Hill, a run-down Adventist preacher from Minnesota, had journeyed to the Battle Creek Sanitarium in May 1884. En route, a fellow traveler had warned him he would get nothing to eat there but bran bread. Hill replied: "I am willing to eat bran bread or any other kind of bread that will make me well again." Upon arrival, he found the strict dietary regimen nothing compared to the hydropathic treatments.

A week's worth of ice-cold baths preceded his first salt glow. Then came the "electric bath." As he lay in tepid water, an "electrician" applied current to his chest and extremities. It seemed to the old man, worn out by many years of itinerant preaching on the frontier, that he was being "rejuvenated" by the electricity.

The treatments experienced by Hill were some of the scores of different baths, showers, enemas, douches and other hydropathic techniques available to Sanitarium patients. Seventh-Day Adventist prophetess Ellen G. White had received a vision concerning the healing properties of water following a convalescence at a Dansville, New York, health spa operated by Dr. James Caleb Jackson.

Upon returning to her Battle Creek church headquarters she decreed the establishment of a similar institution. In 1866, the Western Health Reform Institute opened in a converted farmhouse located just west of the Battle Creek city limits. The Adventists offered vegetarian meals and plenty of water inside and out as an alternative to the drugs advocated by medical doctors.

Despite backing by Sister White's growing church, the institute's ascetic fare and cold baths appealed to few. It lacked a promoter with genuine medical credentials. In 1876, Dr. John Harvey Kellogg arrived to salvage the floundering operation.

Born in 1852, one of 16 children sired by Adventist stalwart John Preston Kellogg, by the age of 10 Kellogg had decided to become a doctor. Sister White and husband James White agreed to help finance his education. He attended the State Normal at Ypsilanti, the University of Michigan and Bellevue Hospital Medical College in New York City where he graduated in 1875. Although he planned a more traditional medical career, the Whites convinced Kellogg to serve as superintendent of the Western Health Reform Institute for one year. He stayed on, however, for the next 67 years, and in the process, built a world-renowned medical institution.

A five-foot, three-inch dynamo of energy, Kellogg set to work with a flourish. He renamed the institute the Battle Creek Sanitarium, a term he had invented, and launched a hectic building campaign that in two years resulted in a huge, four-story mansard building wrapped with 600 feet of veranda. By 1881, a staff of 80 doctors, nurses, cooks, masseurs and bath attendants catered to a rapidly growing clientele.

Kellogg also supplemented traditional water cures with other unusual therapeutic procedures. He thought electricity a good complement to hydrotherapy. He shocked some patients with "sinusoidal current" applications, for example, which made their muscles jerk in a most beneficial manner. Others got jolts of static electricity, a la Frankenstein, while standing in a circular wire cage. Electric light baths somehow made use of the healing properties of incandescent light bulbs.

The inventive doctor also harnessed electricity to operate a variety of fiendish mechanical exercising devices including vibrating machines, power body benders and a pioneer form of the bucking horse that President "Silent Cal" Coolidge later favored for exercise. Those able enough partook of medical gymnastics known as the "Swedish movement cure" or turned out for morning and afternoon sessions of group calisthenics. Men girded their loins in a special diaper that allowed freer movement to play ball, jog or chop wood. Ladies enjoyed more sedate "walking parties."

Food reform became a specialty of Kellogg. Seated on specially designed Sanitarium chairs that promoted good posture, patients ordered from long menus featuring his exotic health food creations. Savita, protose and nuttolene, which one guest compared to shoemaker's paste, were meat substitutes. Kellogg also invented over the course of his career granola, peanut butter and corn flakes as health foods. A Sanitarium cooking school and wife Ella's popular cookbooks also extolled right eating.

Younger brother W.K. Kellogg, who worked as an underpaid henchman at the Sanitarium for 20 years, eventually struck out on his own and turned the health-food business into a commercial success.

Although the doctor continued to believe that the Kellogg signature on corn flakes boxes should have been his own, he continued with his less profitable but more flamboyant medical preoccupations. He saw faulty digestive systems as the cause of "more deaths than all other causes combined." He waged a relentless battle for colon reform, advocating consumption of acidophilus milk, yogurt and other substances in order to alter his countrymen's "intestinal flora."

In 1902, fire leveled the main Sanitarium Building, but Kellogg soon constructed a six-story fireproof structure able to accommodate more than 1,000 patients. He also took over a rival fieldstone hospital in 1911 as an annex. By 1920 the "San" had treated 143,643 patients since 1876.

During the roaring '20s Battle Creek became a mecca for the world's well-heeled run-down. In 1928, a new, 15-story "Central Building" dominated Battle Creek's skyline. Ambulatory guests enjoyed a dance promenade on the San's roof each evening, known as the "hop on the top." By 1930 the Sanitarium staff of 1,800 catered to some 15,000 patients each year who checked in for their "health inventory."

The Depression brought a rapid decline in paying patients, however, and the Sanitarium went into receivership in 1933. It struggled on under more austere conditions until World War II when the U.S. Army purchased the main Sanitarium for use as Percy Jones General Hospital. Colorful Dr. Kellogg died in 1943 at the age of 91.

Early morning calisthenics at the San were a real "eye-opener." (Photo courtesy Michigan Room, Willard Public Library)

Dr. Protar, Backwoods Saint with a Mysterious Past

"Dr." Feodor Protar on Beaver Island. (Photo courtesy Beaver Island Historical Society)

Take equal parts of Albert Schweitzer and Henry David Thoreau, add a dash of the Count of Monte Cristo and a dollop of Don Quixote. What do you get? Dr. Fedor Protar, a backwoods saint with a mysterious past.

Scion of an illustrious scientific family, a highly educated aristocrat, a gifted actor and a talented journalist, at the age of 55, Protar suddenly renounced worldly success to spend his remaining 32 years living as a hermit while ministering to the medical needs of his neighbors on remote Beaver Island.

He was born Friedrich Piers von Parrot on March 6, 1838, in Dorpat (now Tartu) in what was then the Russian Baltic province of Livonia. His grandfather, Friedrich von Parrot, a professor of physics at Dorpat University, had conducted experiments that paved the way for the theories of osmosis, dialysis and galvanic electricity.

His father, Friedrich von Parrot, the younger, carved out an equally illustrious career. He conducted numerous scientific expeditions to measure land elevations and sea levels, becoming the first person to scale Mt. Ararat and several other rugged peaks. Unfortunately, following an expedition to the North Cape to study pendulums and magnetism, he grew ill and died in 1840. He left his widow, Emilie, and a small pension with which she managed to raise young Friedrich and his two older brothers.

Fritz, as his family called him, had a difficult time in grade school. When he was eight, his mother lamented to her diary, "He has my flightiness." Nevertheless, he graduated from preparatory school in 1857, then began a six-year course of study in civil engineering at the Dresden Polytechnic Institute.

But instead of becoming an engineer, shortly after graduation from college he launched a career as a professional actor. Taking the stage name Piers, he wandered throughout Europe appearing in lead roles "not without success." He also wrote, chiefly about theatre reform, and began directing. Piers married and in 1869 settled down as artistic director at the Riga (Latvia city theatre. The five years he served as director are considered some of the best in the history of the Riga theatre.

But one morning in 1874, Parrot left home to attend a rehearsal at the theatre, and that was the last time his wife ever saw him. For some unknown reason, he boarded an immigrant ship that arrived in New York City three weeks later. In America he took the name Fedor (variously spelled Feodor, Feodora, etc.) Protar.

For a while Protar continued his acting career in America, playing leading roles in German in both New York and St. Louis in 1875-76. Then he turned to newspaper work in Chicago and San Antonio, Texas. In 1882, he purchased the *Volkszeitung*, a German newspaper in Rock Island, Illinois. The paper prospered under his editorship.

While on a Great Lakes vacation cruise, Protar first visited Beaver Island, probably in 1890. Located 30 miles northwest of Charlevoix, Beaver Island had enjoyed a brief period of notoriety in the 1850s as the site of James Jesse Strang's Mormon kingdom. Following Strang's assassination and the expulsion of the Mormons in 1856, it had reverted to a wilderness paradise sparsely inhabited by fishermen, farmers, and woodcutters, chiefly of Irish descent. Protar fell in love with its natural beauty and isolated setting.

In 1893, he suddenly sold his prosperous Rock Island newspaper and purchased for $800 a 200-acre farm located on the northwest side of the 53-square-mile-island. There he intended to begin a new life, where, freed from the turmoil of civilization he could concentrate on achieving inner peace.

Originally intending to make his living as a farmer Protar brought with him three horses and implements.

But after dissension with a man he had hired to help him farm, Protar gave up on that idea. Instead, by carefully budgeting the remainder of the money he had received for his newspaper, he was able to follow a solitary and ascetic life style. In tune with his new-found freedom, he allowed his hair and beard their own liberty of growth.

He moved into an abandoned log house originally constructed in 1858, which, after his first uncomfortable winter, he extensively renovated. He planted a few fruit trees, grew garden vegetables, kept chickens and goats, and with the assistance of neighbors raised enough grain for his livestock.

Strangers found Protar secretive and inhospitable, but the islanders, known to this day for their friendliness, soon saw through his gruff and unkempt exterior to the warm and kindly man within. Protar began his medical practice by treating his and neighbor's sick animals. It was a natural step, due in part to the exigencies of the isolated and impoverished community, for him to turn from veterinary to human patients.

Lacking formal medical training, Protar evidently gained his acumen by reading a German-language veterinary guide, a copy of the 1877 edition of the *U.S. Dispensatory*, which listed recipes and dosages for all official medical preparations, and through consultation with his old friend, Dr. Carl Bernhardi of Rock Island. He ordered chemicals and drugs from the mainland, ground powders with his own mortar and pestle, compounded syrups and salves, and dispensed them to those in need. Protar never performed surgery, accepted a fee or payment of any kind, or allowed anyone to call him doctor.

He visited sick families by buggy, sleigh or on foot, offering commonsense advice and simple but effective remedies. Some islanders still recall his dark brown, bitter cough syrup and an equally nasty-tasting gargle for sore throat. Both worked wonders. Others remember the peppermints and horehound candy he always had on hand for children, the apple-flavored drink he carried to men at work, and the many gifts he made of books, clothing and small sums of money.

As Protar grew older, he traveled less. Nevertheless his practice continued strong as the sick showed up at his humble home. A ledger he kept from 1915 to 1925 listed some 2,000 patients he had treated.

Protar died on March 3, 1925, three days short of his 87th birthday. The islanders buried him on his farm, erected a fieldstone enclosure around the grave, and in 1928 installed a bronze plaque there featuring his likeness. His tomb and his renovated house stand today as monuments to the beloved and mysterious Dr. Protar, Beaver Island's "heaven-sent friend."

Dr. Protar's Beaver Island home before it was refurbished as a museum. (Photo courtesy Beaver Island Historical Society)

Silver and Gold: The Presidential Election of 1896

Silver-tongued presidential candidate William Jennings Bryan in 1896.

The boys were whooping it up in Seney the night of October 14, 1896. The tough lumber town had not seen such excitement since bad Dan Dunn plugged Steve Harcourt from behind his bar. The cause of all the commotion was a visit by Democratic presidential candidate William Jennings Bryan, silver-tongued champion of the common man.

Actually Bryan's special campaign train was not scheduled to stop in Seney. "The boy orator of the Platte," had put in a long day talking up the issues at Iron Mountain, Ishpeming, Marquette and other western U.P. towns. Bryan was to get some much-needed sleep as the train clacked over the wilderness stretch from Marquette to St. Ignace.

But Seney's strongly Democratic population was not about to lose its chance to see and maybe hear its hero. An armload of railroad torpedoes, explosive warning devices detonated by the train's wheels, had been placed on the Duluth, South Shore and Atlantic Railroad tracks just west of town. The makings of two giant bonfires, well soaked with kerosene, awaited only the sound of the train's whistle.

Unfortunately, station agent W.G. Miller, a zealous Republican, was wise to the plot. He had wired Marquette, warning the trainmen to ignore the sound of the torpedoes.

The crowd, including a number of well-liquored lumberjacks, waited in the dark at the Seney depot. It was nearly midnight when they heard the engine's whistle followed by the popping of the torpedoes.

The bonfires flared as the train roared into town. Mistaking a porter who stuck his head out the window for the candidate, the crowd yelled, "Hurrah for William Jennings Bryan!" Seconds later the disappointed Democrats watched the back lights of the caboose twinkle into the night.

Then the husky voice of a big lumberjack boomed out,

"To hell with William Jennings Bryan! Lets get a drink!" Needless to say, Bryan lost Schoolcraft County, in which Seney is located, by a wide margin.

Born in Salem, Illinois on March 19, 1860, Bryan grew up to become a lawyer, handsome, charismatic, deeply religious but poor as a church mouse. In 1887 he moved to Lincoln, Nebraska, where he became active in the Democratic Party. His district elected him to Congress in 1890 and 1892. Defeated in a bid for a Senate seat in 1894, he plied his remarkable oratorial powers on the Chautauqua platform, thus enhancing his growing reputation as a spokesman for the people.

In 1896, the dominant national issue was gold and silver. The value of silver had been steadily depreciating since the discovery of the Western Comstock lode in 1859. By 1890 its market value in relation to gold had dropped to a ratio of 20 to one. 1893 brought a national depression triggered in part by an unfavorable U.S. balance of world trade and consequent drain on federal gold reserves. The have-nots, particularly Southern and Midwestern farmers, seized on silver as a panacea for their economic woes. Bryan rose up as a champion of the silver Democrats who called for the free and unlimited coinage of silver at a ratio of 16 to one gold. This would have inflated U.S. currency, making it easier for debtors to pay loans. Bankers, employers and most Republicans naturally favored the strict gold standard.

At the Democratic National Convention held in July 1896, Bryan electrified the delegates with the most inspiring oration of his career, ending with: "You shall not press down upon the brow of labor this crown of thorns, you shall not crucify mankind upon a cross of gold." His ideas were simplistic, his rhetoric often meaningless, but then as now it was not what you said but how you said it that won votes. Bryan clinched the nomination with his "cross of gold" speech and a group of gold Democrats bolted from the party.

Similarly, some silver Republicans who represented Western mining states left their party to back Bryan after the regular Republicans nominated William McKinley of Ohio. Cleveland industrialist Mark Hanna masterminded McKinley's campaign. He raised an enormous campaign chest and broadcast a torrent of political tracts across the nation while McKinley waged a decorous contest from the porch of his Canton, Ohio home.

But Bryan carried his battle to the people in the most vigorous presidential campaign America had ever seen. He traveled 18,000 miles by rail to deliver more than 600 formal speeches in 10 weeks. Five million Americans thrilled to the rich timbre of his voice.

In late August, Bryan stumped through the southern tier of Michigan counties. Then beginning October 14, he launched a four-day whirlwind sweep through the peninsulas. Following his flit through Seney he headed south, addressing large crowds at Traverse City and Big Rapids. At Grand Rapids he delivered three orations, one to an audience entirely of women. While yet banned from the ballot box, the ladies showed their approval by presenting Mrs. Bryan with "a handsome badge made 16 parts of silver and one of gold."

On October 16, Bryan talked from early morning until midnight, delivering 25 speeches in 19 cities. In Kalamazoo, Celery City boomers did some campaigning of their own by presenting Bryan with a case of the crunchy vegetables.

On the final day of his Michigan tour Bryan drew large crowds at Flint, Bay City and Detroit. He told the Flint audience: "One of your bankers called a farmer into his room and said to him 'If Bryan is elected President, I shall foreclose the mortgage on your farm.' The farmer replied, 'If McKinley is elected you can have the farm, because I will not be able to pay it, but if Bryan is elected you cannot foreclose the mortgage because under bimetallism I will be able to pay it off.'"

The election of 1896 had, in fact, become a class war. Manufacturers warned employees that if Bryan won, factories would close down; bankers told depositors the banks would fail; and some business contracts were made contingent on McKinley's election. In Michigan the Republican party bosses ran popular Detroit Mayor Hazen Pingree for governor, although they thoroughly hated his liberalism, in hopes of carrying the state for McKinley on his coattails.

The various tactics took their toll. Bryan lost Michigan by roughly 56,000 votes. McKinley won the campaign with a comfortable electoral margin. "Bryan, Bryan, Bryan, candidate for president who sketched a silver Zion," ran again in 1900 and 1908, losing by greater margins each time.

Presidential candidate William Jennings Bryan regales a crowd in 1896.

Round Oak Stoves, They Warmed the Nation

The celebrated Round Oak stove.

Folks in four counties set their watches by the deep bass voice of the Round Oak Stove Company's whistle, which bellowed out its summons to work at 6:45 six mornings a week. In the Cass County community of Dowagiac, an army of laborers, sometimes 1,500 strong, hitched up their galluses, grabbed tin lunch buckets and made beelines for the massive stove works sprawled over 15 acres at the heart of the city.

In 1899, they cast 40 tons of pig iron a day into fire pots, shaped boiler plate into stove bodies and decorated them with finely worked, nickel-plated fittings. Millions of Round Oak heaters, furnaces and kitchen ranges flowed by rail to homes across the country, making Dowagiac a household word. Few of the city's 4,500 residents in 1899 did not owe some portion of their well-being to the stove factory.

Philo D. Beckwith, an entrepreneur from Battle Creek who arrived at the recently platted village in 1854, founded the firm that for nearly seven decades dominated Dowagiac's economy. Beckwith purchased a machine shop, added a foundry and eked out a livelihood as a blacksmith and manufacturer of iron novelties.

Beckwith also had a hand in developing Dowagiac's other major industry - the manufacture of mechanical grain drills. He marketed the nation's pioneer horse-drawn roller grain drill, which revolutionized the planting of field crops.

In the 1860s, Beckwith invented an improved "under-draft" wood-burning stove to heat his shop. His stove featured a smaller door for ash removal and other innovations that made the fire compartment more airtight and hence more efficient. Michigan Central Railroad officials noticed the superior heating qualities of one of Beckwith's stoves that had been installed in the Dowagiac Depot and ordered more for other locations. By 1868, Beckwith had constructed a larger factory adjacent to the railroad tracks and hired eight foundrymen.

Beckwith's high-quality stoves proved so popular that he patented the design in 1873 and eventually dropped production of grain rollers to manufacture "Round Oak" stoves exclusively. Over the next two decades, Beckwith expanded his factory almost yearly to keep up with the booming business. In 1886, he added a furnace to his line and later a popular Round Oak kitchen range. The focal point of Victorian households on cold winter days, cheerfully glowing Round Oak stoves brought comfort to millions from coast to coast. Ultimately, more than 400 competitors emulated the Round Oak design.

In 1878, Fred E. Lee, a Dowagiac native, married Beckwith's daughter Kate. The following year, he joined his father-in-law's burgeoning business. When Beckwith died in 1889, Lee took over as general manager. He and Kalamazoo lawyer William G. Howard continued to operate the company under the title "P.D. Beckwith's Estate."

Beckwith had been a generous donor to the community and a patron of the theatre in particular. So his family members decided to apply some of his large estate toward the construction of a memorial theatre. Dowagiac watched in awe as a massive three-story Romanesque structure, built with Lake Superior red sandstone, took shape. A large stone image of Beckwith crowned the center of the front facade, and a series of busts of celebrated actresses, playwrights, composers and philosophers gazed out from the cornice line.

Lee instructed the interior designers to spare no expense. The finished building gained the reputation as "the finest theatre in America." Col. Robert Ingersoll, "the great agnostic," whose own stone likeness was incorporated into the facade along with those of Voltaire, Thomas Paine and Walt Whitman, helped dedicate the Beckwith Memorial Theatre Building in January 1893.

Over the succeeding decades, such notables as Jenny Lind, John Drew and Ethel Barrymore appeared on the opulent stage. The structure also housed the Dowagiac post office, the City Council chambers, Lee's bank and the Round Oak Stove Company office.

As the 20th century dawned, Dowagiac billed itself as "The Furnace City of America." In 1905, the company began using a mythological Indian chief it named Doe-Wah-Jack as its trademark. Colorful calendars portraying the chief fighting bears and in other ticklish situations, souvenir spoons, plates and steins as well as decorations on the stoves made Doe-Wah-Jack nearly as familiar as the Indian on the buffalo nickel.

In 1925, the company proclaimed that over two million of its stoves were in use. The Round Oak line had grown to encompass the traditional Square Base Heating Stove; the Duplex Heater; the Romal, Chief, Ironbilt, Porcelain and Combination Ranges, which burned gas, wood or coal; and the Moistair, Ironbilt and Pipeless Heating Systems. The company also established its own enameling plant to produce the porcelain trim on its popular kitchen ranges.

But the failure to adapt to changing times and stiff competition from less durable but cheaper brands ultimately spelled doom for the mammoth factory. After acquisition by the Kaiser-Fraser Company during World War II, no more stoves, ranges or furnaces were produced, although the company did manufacture Round Oak water heaters for a few more years. Ultimately it joined the roster of defunct Michigan heating manufacturers, including Detroit's Garland, Battle Creek's A B Stove Co., the Holland Furnace Co., and the Kalamazoo Stove Co.

The majestic Beckwith Theatre fell victim to the wrecking ball in 1966. Fifteen of the stone sculptures ended up at nearby Southwestern Michigan College, where a museum of Round Oak memorabilia has been established.

The Merry Oldsmobile

This 1906 model "Merry Oldsmobile" sold for $650.

The little curved-dash Oldsmobile that putted along New York City's Fifth Avenue and Roy D. Chapin, a 21-year-old test driver who gripped its tiller, were both well-spattered with mud and oil. It was November 5, 1901, and Chapin had just guided the vehicle over the 835-mile course from Detroit. The trip, on roads so miserable that Chapin had opted to drive along the tow path of the Erie Canal for part of the distance, had taken 7½ days. He had spent a good deal of that time patching tires, repairing the transmission, springs, axles and steering, as well as replacing the one-cylinder engine's gaskets, which repeatedly blew out under the strain of going uphill.

Chapin was within a mile of his destination when a pedestrian stepped out in front of him. He slammed on his brakes and the Oldsmobile spun around on the slippery brick pavement, hit the curb and broke several spokes on its bicycle-type wheels. The vehicle wobbled the final distance at a slower pace.

He pulled up before the ritzy Waldorf-Astoria Hotel on 34th Street, shut off his engine and bounded toward the door. But the doorman took one look at the battered little runabout and the driver's grimy appearance and turned him away. Chapin gained entrance through the servants' entrance in the rear of the hotel and soon located the room where his boss, Ransom E. Olds, who had wisely taken the train to New York, nervously paced the floor.

Born in Geneva, Ohio, in 1864, the man whose name would be forever linked with automotive pioneering had spent his early life on the farm of his father, Pliny. Olds learned to detest the endless hours of mindless drudgery demanded by farm life. He particularly hated the very smell of horses. Ironically, his later automotive achievements would do much to remove them from the nation's thoroughfares.

In 1880, the Olds family moved to Lansing where Pliny

established a machine shop that specialized in manufacturing small steam engines. Ransom dropped out of school in the 10th grade to work as a bookkeeper and machinist in his father's shop. In 1885, he became a partner in the firm of P.F. Olds and Son.

Two years later Olds tested his first automobile, a three-wheeled rig powered by one of the firm's gasoline-fired steam engines. By 1892 he had constructed a superior model that utilized two small steam engines mounted over the rear wheels. An article on his contraption in the *Scientific American* so impressed a London-based patent medicine firm that it purchased the vehicle for use in a branch office in India. That event marked the first sale and the first overseas shipment of a Michigan-made automobile.

Olds then turned from steam to the wave of the future, the gasoline-fueled internal combustion engine. He secured a patent for his Olds Safety Gas and Vapor engine in 1896 and also installed one of his engines in a third automobile prototype that year. Booming sales for the improved Olds engine spurred a new addition to the plant and in 1897 the company was reorganized as the Olds Gasoline Engine Works. Olds also convinced a group of local investors to create a separate company to manufacture automobiles. The Olds engine operation worked feverishly the next few years to keep up with the backlog of orders for its popular product, but the Olds automobile company faltered due to labor troubles, insufficient production space and lack of funds. By 1900 the firm had produced only six vehicles.

When Lansing investors refused to risk more funds on something as unlikely as an automobile, Olds looked elsewhere. Samuel L. Smith, a retired copper magnate, agreed to finance an automobile factory if Olds would relocate to Detroit and involve Smith's two unemployed sons in the business. So in early 1900 a modern new facility on Jefferson Avenue near Belle Isle went into production of an "improved model" that sold for $1,250. But few sold and Olds dissipated his energies by experimenting with 11 different models, including some powered by electricity.

Then he had a brainstorm. Sometime in the summer or early fall of 1900 Olds sat down in the office of Horace Loomis, a bright young engineer on his staff, and drew some rough sketches of a new model. He told Loomis "What we want to build is a small, low-down runabout that will have a shop cost of around $300 and will sell for $650." By October the Olds staff had designed the prototype of the automobile that would revolutionize the industry - the curved-dash Oldsmobile.

Weighing only 580 pounds, it was steered by a tiller and powered by a little, one-cylinder engine mounted under the body. The aerodynamic curved front was developed for eye appeal and to divert a flow of air to the radiator located in the footboard. Olds launched a national publicity campaign to market his new product. "Nothing to watch but the road," his company slogan assured customers. Despite one owner's quip that "he got tired of watching the same stretch of road all the time," the vehicle's lightness, reliability and especially its price appealed to Americans and hundreds of orders flowed in for Olds' runabout.

But on March 9, 1901, while Olds was vacationing in California, his Detroit plant burned to the ground. The night watchman was able to wheel one curved-dash Oldsmobile out of the factory before the roof and walls caved in. But the disaster proved a blessing in disguise when Olds decided to devote all his facilities to production of that one model.

Sensing an opportunity to lure Olds back to his hometown, the Lansing Business Men's Association raised funds to purchase a 52-acre plat formerly used as a fairgrounds and offered it free as a site for a new Oldsmobile plant. That offer, as well as the fact that the prevailing wage scale in Lansing was one-third less than in Detroit brought Olds back. By the end of 1901, more than 400 Oldsmobiles had rolled out of the new Lansing plant. Olds also rebuilt his Detroit factory at which other Oldsmobiles were constructed.

The second annual automobile show held in Madison Square Garden in November 1901, to which Chapin had made his epic trip, also proved a milestone in Oldsmobile history. Olds had the battered little vehicle polished up and placed on display. It attracted a good deal of attention at the show, including an order for 1,000 vehicles from one dealer.

In 1902, the company built 2,500 Oldsmobiles, followed by 4,000 the next year. But in 1904, Olds resigned as a result of a feud with the Smiths over company management. Within months he had established another company in Lansing that produced Reo (his initials) cars and trucks.

The curved-dash model, popularized as the "Merry Oldsmobile" by songwriter Gus Edwards, became the industry's first mass-produced automobile. It remained in production through 1906. Two years later the company Olds had founded became part of General Motors. Oldsmobile remains America's oldest automotive brand name still in production.

Dr. Peebles Sucked a Pebble and Never Stuttered Again!

Dr. James M. Peebles, spiritualist, physician and bunco artist, in 1871.

The veins in District Attorney William D. Gordon's neck bulged when he bellowed at the defendant: "Do you, before this jury of God-fearing men now claim, under oath, that you have the powers of our Lord and Saviour Jesus Christ, to heal the sick and restore the dead to life?"

A hush fell over the Detroit District Courtroom. Dr. James M. Peebles of Battle Creek calmly rose from the chair. A six-foot four-inch giant of a man sporting a long white beard that flowed over the lapels of his expensive black suit, Peebles looked very much like a biblical patriarch. Raising a clenched fist high above his head, Peebles thundered in a rich baritone voice: "I do! I do! And may God strike me dead on this spot if I am not possessed of such power! He gave it to me. Speak O God, and give this jury the proof! The proof!"

Peebles stood silent for nearly a minute, as the tense courtroom waited for divine retribution. Then he relaxed and turning to the jury murmured softly: "Gentlemen, you see for yourselves."

And they did see, on that day in 1901, and they heard - enough to convict the old charlatan of medical fraud. But that slap on the wrist would be but a temporary and soon-forgotten setback for the career of one of Michigan's most flamboyant flimflammers.

Born March 23, 1822, in Whitingham, Vermont, the eldest of seven siblings, at a young age Peebles moved with his family to western New York. His early ambitions, wrote his biographer, "ran in the channel of the brooks, full of babbles and frolics." He had a miserable time in the one-room schoolhouse he walked to largely because he stuttered. But a local professor cured the problem by having him talk with a pebble under the point of his tongue. Freed of his speech impediment, Peebles soon developed a remarkable oratorical style.

At the age of 20 he became a Universalist minister and thereby honed his pulpit skills. In 1856, he chanced to share a Cleveland hotel room with the celebrated traveling mediums, the Davenport Brothers. Peebles ridiculed their craft, but later that night he saw the light. Spirits rocked his bed, buffeted him around the room and an angelic voice announced "you are appointed for a great work; gird up your loins, buckle on your sandals, grasp the sword of truth. Go forth." Peebles girded himself in a black suit and two months later rode into Battle Creek, long legs dangling below the stirrups, to take charge of the local Spiritualist Church.

Despite the fact that Battle Creek had become a Midwestern center for the "rappers," as Spiritualists were sometimes called, Peebles faced a community of "doubting Thomases." He changed all that in 1858 when he teamed up with an itinerant mesmerist to stage a demonstration of his powers.

The pair got a heckler to volunteer for a hypnotic experiment. Once under "magnetic sleep," his hand moved as if in writing. Given a pen and paper, he scribbled what appeared to be gibberish "in an unknown tongue." But when Peebles held it before a mirror it read: "I was killed on the Great Western Railroad near Hamilton, Canada, two hours ago. I have a wife and two children in Buffalo. John Morgan."

When the next day's papers corroborated Morgan's death, Peebles garnered plenty of new disciples. The hypnotised heckler also launched his own career as a traveling medium.

About that time Peebles started up a psychic sideline, healing through the agency of his personal spirit contact, who turned out to be none other than Chief Powhatan, of colonial Virginia fame. Powhatan, as Peebles told his patients, taught him certain ancient Indian herbal remedies that he was only too happy to share with them - for a fee, that is. But even with his pipeline to the hereafter, Peebles evidently found it hard to make ends meet in Battle Creek. He wandered off to

California in 1860, landed back in Battle Creek 18 months later, and in 1867 moved on to greener pastures in New Jersey.

Out East, Peebles began plying his pen, first by editing a Spiritualist hymn book. Then he wrote a long series of volumes including: *The Christ Question Settled; Hell Revised, Modernized and Made More Comfortable; Vaccination a Curse and a Menace to Personal Liberty;* and *Death Defeated, or the Psychic Secrets of How to Keep Young.*

In 1869, for some unknown reason, President Ulysses Grant appointed him consul to Trebinzonde, a Turkish Black Sea port. He stayed at that post only briefly, however, before commencing a series of around-the-world travels during which he studied "the laws, customs, and religions of nations and people, giving special attention to spiritualism, magic and theosophy."

Peebles paused briefly from his travels to pick up a quick medical degree from a fraudulent Philadelphia diploma mill in 1876. Dr. Peebles then set up a series of psychic healing institutes in New Jersey, Texas and California. But Battle Creek beckoned him back, and in 1896 the 73-year-old white-bearded giant launched Dr. Peebles Institute at 350 Madison Street under the motto "Health is the foundation of success" - his own continued success, he hoped.

At his institute, Peebles allied himself with a husband-and-wife team, Dr. J.A. and Bertha Burroughs. Dr. Burroughs focused his occult powers to "determine the secret cause of chronic disease." Bertha handled ladies "who preferred the counsul of their own sex in certain matters." Peebles himself tackled particularly tough cases. Patients unable to visit the institute needed only to jot down their symptoms on a special form, mail it - with prepayment - to Battle Creek and the psychic team posted back a diagnosis and cure. Use of the U.S. mail for his medical chicanery evidently landed him in the U.S. District Court in Detroit in 1901.

Following that embarrassment, Peebles shifted from mail-order diagnosis to a carefully worded patent-medicine racket. He and his new partner, W.T. Bobo, M.D., former proprietor of a mail-order goiter cure, launched a national advertising campaign under the bold-faced headline "Fits" to market their double-barreled cure, a "brain restorative" and "nerve tonic." But when Pure Food and Drug Act chemists took the liberty of analyzing the mixtures, they found them to be an alcoholic tincture flavored with bitter almonds, and promptly fined Peebles again.

By 1915 Peebles had joined the California medical community, a haven for eccentric practitioners. In 1922, Peebles, who earlier had authored the best seller, *How to Live a Century and Grow Old Gracefully*, died one month short of his 100th birthday.

Dr. Peebles' epilepsy cure, guaranteed to relieve you - of your money, that is.

"Hurry Up" Yost and the First Rose Bowl Game

Fielding H. Yost, who gave the term "hurry-up" a new meaning.

"Hurry up; football is a game of hurry, hurry, hurry," he wrote. "Hurry up and be the first man to line up."

"Hurry up and get into every play. Football is played by eleven men. Spectators are not wanted on the field; their place is in the grand stand," he shouted to his players in practice.

"Hurry up" Yost, a Detroit reporter dubbed him. That was in 1901, his first season as University of Michigan football coach. His Wolverines would crush every team they played that year and climax their season with an overwhelming victory in the first Rose Bowl game.

That launched Michigan's golden era of the gridiron. During his first five seasons, Yost's "point a minute" teams would score an amazing 2,821 points to opponents 42. They would win 55 games and tie one before finally being beaten by the University of Chicago 2-0, thus compiling an intercollegiate football undefeated streak that has yet to be bettered.

Born in Fairview, West Virginia on April 30, 1871, the son of a Confederate veteran, Fielding Harris Yost worked as a deputy sheriff in his hometown before enrolling in the Normal School at nearby Fairmont in 1889. He also secured a teaching job at $30 per month before transferring to Ohio Normal at Ada, Ohio, the following fall. There he played first base on the baseball team for two years and got his first introduction to a rough-and-tumble variety of football, played with as many as 200 opponents on the field.

But teaching, and in particular the low wages paid teachers in those days, did not appeal to Yost. He returned to Fairview to work in his father's general store. An oil boom hit West Virginia about that time and Yost decided a knowledge of property leases and mineral rights would be valuable.

In 1895 he enrolled in the West Virginia University Law School at Morgantown. He played guard and left tackle on the football team there. His team won all but one game his first season.

By the time he received his law degree in 1897, football had become his true love. That fall he got a job coaching Ohio Wesleyan University. His team tied the University of Michigan and beat Ohio State. The following year Yost coached the Cornhuskers at the University of Nebraska to a winning season. He led the University of Kansas team to an undefeated record in 1899.

Anxious to see other parts of the country, Yost accepted a coaching position at Stanford University in 1900. In his spare time, he also coached the Stanford freshman team, the San Jose College team, the football team at San Francisco's Lowell High School and, during a deer hunting trip, the Ukiah High School eleven. All five teams won championships.

But the following year Stanford implemented a policy that required its football coach to be an alumnus and Yost was out of a job. When Charles Baird, University of Michigan manager of athletics, learned Yost was available, he wrote him in part: "Our people are greatly roused up over the defeats of the past two years, and a great effort will be made... Would you care to coach in Ann Arbor?" Yost forwarded a huge scrapbook documenting his football accomplishments and boarded a train for Ann Arbor. He soon signed a contract paying him $2,300 and living expenses, about twice the salary of a full professor.

The U of M got its money's worth that first season. Yost's dynamic coaching was coupled with an exceptionally talented roster, including Harrison "Boss" Weeks from Allegan at quarterback, fullback and defensive end Neil Snow, linemen George Gregory, Bruce Shorts, Don McGugin and Everett Sweeley and halfback Al Herrnstein. Yost also recruited a freshman he had coached at San Jose, William Martin "Willie" Heston, who would dazzle Michigan fans during the succeeding four years and in the process win gridiron immortality.

The Wolverines drubbed Albion College 50-0 in the opening game of the season and the next nine teams fell likewise. The highly touted University of Buffalo suffered the most humiliating defeat in its history 128-0. The final season's tally was Michigan 501 points - opponents 0.

Football, as played in 1901, was a far cry from the modern game. Some of the rules undoubtedly helped Yost's team rack up such phenomenal scores. The team that scored last, for example, could elect to receive the next kickoff. The forward pass was illegal, but a team could retain possession of the ball by making only five yards in three downs. A field goal counted the same as a touchdown, five points. The game was longer, with two 35-minute halves and no quarter time-outs, but so was the field, 110 yards from goal to goal. Officials called tripping as a penalty, but clipping was perfectly allowable. Uniforms bore no numbers and were equipped with sewn-in quilted padding. Helmets without face masks were optional and if worn could not be made of hard material. Players wore their locks long to help cushion the shock of impact, and thereby started a hair fashion craze.

The national excitement over football, in fact, spurred James R.H. Wagner, newly elected president of the Tournament of Roses Association and a former Michigan resident, to invite the Wolverines to play a football game following the Rose Parade. The gala tournament that originated in 1886 had previously featured polo matches.

University officials gave Yost permission to play the game providing the association paid all expenses and a $3-per-day meal allowance for each team member. The train carrying Yost and 15 players reached San Francisco on December 24 and two days later the team started down the coast to Los Angeles.

Approximately 8,000 fans turned out to watch the Wolverines play Stanford, the strongest team on the Pacific Coast, on New Years Day 1902. The temperature stood at 85 degrees and the playing field was dry and dusty. The first 12 minutes of the game proved uneventful, then Yost's hurry-up strategy began to pay off. Despite the heat and unfamiliar terrain, the Michigan players proved themselves in better condition for the fast-paced game. They led 17-0 at half time. Eight minutes before the end of the contest with the score at 49-0, the Stanford captain asked to terminate the game.

The following year the Rose Bowl Association decided to substitute chariot races for the football exhibition. Not until 1916 would another Rose Bowl football game be held.

Yost and his teams enjoyed many other victorious seasons during the 25 years he served as head football coach. Yost nevertheless marred his remarkable career with racial prejudice. No black athlete ever played on his team. Yost also held the position of university director of athletics from 1921 until his retirement in 1941.

But Yost never saw his beloved Wolverines play in another Rose Bowl. He died on August 20, 1946. On January 1, 1948, Michigan played its second Rose Bowl. Amazingly, the Wolverines defeated Southern California by the identical score of 49-0.

Booker T. Washington Finds His People's Promised Land

Samuel Hawkes was proud to be the largest taxpayer in Calvin Township, Cass County, in 1902.

The buggy carrying Booker T. Washington pulled up before the African Methodist Church in Cass County's rural Calvin Township. A crowd of several hundred black residents and a brass band had assembled to greet their distinguished visitor. Tired and dusty from his 10-hour inspection tour of the township, he nevertheless was cajoled into delivering a short address. Based on what he had experienced that day, Washington must have thought he had finally found his people's promised land.

Calvin Township had been pioneered during the 1830s, in part by a group of Quakers. Courageous anti-slavery activists, the Quakers operated an important underground railroad station there. Their tolerance also moved some runaway slaves to seek permanent sanctuary within the township. Beginning in the 1840s, increasing numbers of free black families, originally from Virginia and North Carolina, immigrated to this haven to take advantage of the cheap farmland then on the market.

In 1847, for example, Sampson Saunders, a wealthy planter in what is now West Virginia, left provisions in his will that his slaves were to be emancipated. He also provided $15,000 for them to establish a new life in the North. The executors of the will purchased a plat of land in Calvin Township, and a few days before Christmas 1849, 46 men, women and children, including an 80-year-old woman, arrived in the land of freedom. Following the custom of adopting the surname of their former master, or an approximate spelling of the name, most of the former slaves took the names Saunders or Sanders. Their descendants still live in Cass County.

In 1864, the state census taker counted 989 "colored persons" in the township, two-thirds of its entire population. Over the decades some farmers failed and the bright lights of the cities lured young people away. Washington, during his visit in August 1902, found 759 blacks and 512 whites living in Calvin Township.

Booker Taliaferro Washington, born a slave on a Virginia plantation in 1858, worked his way through school as a coal miner and janitor. Following graduation from Hampton Institute in Virginia in 1875, he taught. In 1881 he began organizing a school for blacks at Tuskegee, Alabama. At Tuskegee Institute he emphasized industrial training.

Articulate and a commanding public speaker, Washington became the principle spokesman for American blacks. He advocated gradual betterment of the black race through its own labors. Rather than relying on legislation to achieve equality, he urged blacks to distinguish themselves in their various occupations and thereby win the respect of the white power structure. More militant black leaders such as W.E.B. Du Bois and the incipient NAACP, founded in 1909, disagreed with this philosophy, but Washington's personal prestige earned him title as the "national Negro leader."

When Washington learned of the black community in Calvin Township, an apparent demonstration of a successful agrarian economy, he traveled to Cassopolis by rail to examine the situation firsthand.

Cass County Probate Court Judge L.B. Des Voignes drove Washington on a 30-mile tour of the township. Skirting Diamond Lake, they soon reached the township southeast of Cassopolis where Washington found himself passing "well cultivated farms and comfortable looking farm houses" with attractive yards and well-maintained outbuildings.

Washington stopped to observe a large wheat threshing operation. About 20 black laborers operated a powerful steam engine and threshing machine owned by Henry L. Archer, a black entrepreneur. He threshed most of the grain in the township for white farmers as well as blacks.

Most impressive was the story of Samuel Hawkes, who Washington called "a fine specimen of the race."

Hawkes had moved from Virginia via Ohio to Calvin Township in 1853. He had begun working for himself at the age of 16 by cutting cordwood. Nine years later he paid $800 cash for an 80-acre parcel in the township. By the time of Washington's visit, Hawkes was worth over $50,000 and held the distinction of being the top taxpayer in the township.

Of the eight country schoolhouses in the townships, half were staffed by black teachers. The township supervisor, Cornelius Lawson, also was black. When Washington asked Des Voignes about the ability of Calvin Township's blacks to govern themselves, a hotly debated issue of the time, Des Voignes replied that "the affairs of the township were conducted as well politically as any in the county."

What's, more, Calvin's black tax collector was proud of his record of paying to the county treasurer each year his township's taxes before any of the other 35 townships. Once, when a rival township nearly beat the record because of one tardy Calvin Township taxpayer, other Calvin Township residents chipped in to pay his taxes on time.

Probably the most significant item that Washington recorded came as a response to his questions about race relations. Five prominent Cass County officials concurred that the degree of white prejudice against blacks was in direct relationship to their distance from Calvin Township. In other words, whites who had black neighbors and those who dealt with the black farmers as businessmen harbored little or no prejudice. Washington happily reported his findings in an article in *Outlook Magazine* in 1903.

A Bicycle Odyssey
in 1904

*Claude C. Murphey (left) and Clarence M. Darling pose in Jackson at
the start of their amazing bicycle odyssey.*

Trundling their bicycles along the track with one hand and holding torches in the other, the two youths had nearly reached the halfway point of the narrow two-mile-long railroad tunnel that cut through the summit of the Cascade Mountain Range in central Washington. Suddenly they heard a faint rumbling like distant thunder. Straining their eyes into the darkness they spotted a pinprick of light. The light grew bigger and the rumbling louder. With a sickening wave of fear, they realized that a fast freight train was approaching.

They had come too far to make a run for it - their only hope was to press themselves against the tunnel wall. They quickly loosened and removed the handlebars of their bikes, stood them one before the other and squeezed their backs tightly against the rock wall.

Seconds later the blinding light of the locomotive was upon them. With a thundering roar and hiss of steam it passed with but three inches to spare. The long line of freight cars clacked by, then came the roar and hiss of another engine in the middle of the train, another line of cars and finally one last engine in the rear. Choking and coughing in the smoke and soot left by the locomotives, shaking from their ordeal, the youths stumbled on.

That narrow brush with death was but one of many experienced by 19-year-old Clarence M. Darling and 20-year-old Claude C. Murphey of Jackson during a monumental bicycle tour through every state and territory in the continental United States that began in 1904.

The motive for their amazing odyssey was a bet made with the pair by certain eastern sportsmen. The $5,000 wager, however, included some stiff provisions. The trip had to be made by bicycle, the itinerary included stops at specified cities in each state where official verification was required, and it was to be completed within 18 months. Furthermore, the cyclists were to start penniless, neither to beg, work, borrow nor steal, and to make all of their traveling expenses through the sale of small, souvenir aluminum calling card receivers on which was printed a description of the venture.

Darling and Murphey, who had dreamed for years of making a similar trip, leaped at the prospect of winning $5,000, equivalent to 20 times or more that amount in today's currency. The boys carefully planned their strategy, mapped out the best routes and released the story to the local press one week before their projected start. The general consensus in Jackson was that they were "candidates for the Kalamazoo Insane Asylum."

Nevertheless, a small crowd of well-wishers turned out bright and early on the morning of May 2, 1904, for the start. Darling and Murphey had new single-speed bicycles, heavy touring models weighing 28 pounds. Canvas packs secured within the frames of the bicycles, carbide lanterns mounted on the front wheels, repair kits, and other accessories, including a portable typewriter strapped to the handlebars of one, brought the total weight of each machine to 75 pounds.

The riders sported "regulation bicycle suits" including purple and yellow sweaters emblazoned in front with a scarlet YMCA insignia, bright orange bicycle stockings and white elk-hide bicycle shoes. They posed for a final publicity photo in front of the Otsego Hotel on the corner of East Main and Francis Street in downtown Jackson, shook hands all around, then pedaled west, wondering if they would ever again see their native city.

The first day's cycling along the dirt roads to Battle Creek went smoothly. But during the following day's ride they got their first taste of conditions that would plague their entire journey - miserable roads, unsuitable for walking much less bicycling. Between Kalamazoo and Oshtemo the road consisted of eight to nine inches of loose white sand through which they walked and shoved their bicycles with great difficulty.

At Michigan City they left the heavy sand for the relative ease of bumping and walking their bicycles along the railroad tracks. Most of their entire itinerary, in fact, would be spent trundling their bikes along stretches of railroad. High trestles and long tunnels brought several close encounters with speeding locomotives. Once they hung from the girders of a bridge over a deep gorge in Idaho as a train thundered overhead.

In Chicago they experienced an early-morning adventure with a robber, who the youths thwarted by drawing the revolvers they had taken the precaution to pack. Next came a bout with the heavy "gumbo" mud of central Ilinois that clung to their bicycle tires, forcing them to plod along heavy-footed while carrying their machines.

When they could ride, they occasionally made excellent progress. They pedaled the 112 miles from Redfield to Mitchell, South Dakota, in one day, for example, and that included towing one disabled bike behind the other for the last 16 miles.

Repairs were a constant problem. Thorns from hedgerows and cactus spines out West frequently punctured their thin tires. Broken chains, worn bearings and brakes and other equipment failures brought additional delays. While in Texas they had to push their bikes 236 miles out of the way to El Paso to find a mechanic able to mend a broken frame.

The cyclists purchased meals at restaurants or homes en route but were often reduced through lack of funds to subsist on sardines and crackers. Their original plans were to find lodging at cheap hotels or YMCAs, but night sometimes found them many miles from civilization in which case barn lofts or abandoned shacks sufficed.

In crossing the rockies via the railroad track it took them 11 days to make 315 miles. They were down to their last 27 cents when they hit California, but successful sales of their souvenirs there earned them $160. They spent the winter of 1904/05 pushing their bikes for 500 miles in up to two feet of snow while crossing Oklahoma, Kansas, and Missouri.

Next came many days of sloshing through the spring floods they encountered in the Ozarks, the Florida panhandle and other sections of the South. Sales of their "damn Yankee" souvenirs in the South were few and far between. By the time they had worked their way up the Atlantic seaboard to Portland, Maine, their funds had dwindled to $1, which soon went to a bicycle repairman.

They made it into Vermont, which left only three states to pass through. But, unable to sell souvenirs to New Englanders, who told them to get a job, and having gone without food for two days, they were forced to wash dishes for a meal in Burlington, Vermont, a desperate act that lost them the $5,000 prize.

Nevertheless, Darling and Murphey continued on their planned itinerary and arrived back in Jackson on August 11, 1905. The odometers on their battered bicycles registered an amazing 13,407 miles!

Harry Houdini, the World's Greatest Necromancer

Harry Houdini performing a rope escape in 1898.

Cuffed hands held high, Harry Houdini hurtled feet first toward the icy Detroit River. The safety rope tied around his waist whirled off the coil on the Belle Isle Bridge 25 feet above the river. The crowd that lined the bridge gasped in unison as Houdini splashed beneath the water.

It was the noon hour on November 27, 1906, a raw blustery day with the temperature close to the freezing point. Many in the crowd held their collective breath, wondering how long the famous "handcuff king" could survive beneath the frigid water. Then came a cheer as Houdini's head broke the surface. He swam to a waiting rescue boat, slung the handcuffs over the side and scrambled aboard.

Houdini's stunt made the front page of the *Detroit News*, and as a result he enjoyed a packed house during his performance at the Temple Theatre later that afternoon. During the following 20 years Houdini would top his Detroit River plunge with many more death-defying escapes, including a jump into San Francisco Bay with his hands cuffed behind his back and a 75-pound iron ball chained to one ankle.

But the Detroit River stunt became his "most famous single outdoor exploit," not because of what actually happened but because of the exaggerated version of the event that grew wilder and wilder with each telling. Houdini and his wife, Bess, later claimed in print that the Detroit River was frozen over at the time.

Houdini jumped, they said, handcuffed, chained and leg-ironed, off the bridge into a hole that had been chopped in the ice. After he had freed himself, the current had swept him downstream and he had risen beneath the ice unable to find the hole. After five minutes had passed, watching reporters had rushed off to hurry out extra editions containing the news of his drowning.

Bess, ill in her room at the Hotel St. Claire, had heard newsboys shouting that Houdini was dead. Meanwhile, back at the bridge an assistant had lowered a rope into the hole in the ice preparing to swim down after Houdini's body. Suddenly, after eight minutes had passed, Houdini's head shot out of the water gasping for breath. He had survived by breathing a thin layer of air bubbles below the surface of the ice.

Hyperbole aside, Houdini's real-life exploits were unbelievable enough.

He was born Ehrich Weisse in Budapest, Hungary, on March 24, 1874, the son of a rabbi. As a small child he immigrated with his family to Appleton, Wisconsin. The family moved often to various locations in the Milwaukee vicinity and in 1888 to New York City. As a teen-ager, Ehrich worked at a Broadway tie factory where a fellow employee introduced him to magic. He soon acquired a copy of *The Memoirs of Robert Houdin*, "the father of modern magic." Houdin became his idol and in his honor young Ehrich took the stage name Houdini. The "Harry" he borrowed from another famous magician, Harry Thurston.

Houdini began his stage career in a series of New York beer halls. He played at Coney Island, the Bowery, the Columbian Exposition in 1893 and eventually worked his way into the Orpheum vaudeville circuit. From card tricks and other standard illusions he branched into his forte, escapes.

In 1899, he challenged the San Francisco Police Department that he could escape from any restraint they could muster. After thoroughly frisking his body, the police fitted Houdini's ankles in irons, shackled his hands behind his back, linked the chains with ten pairs of handcuffs and carried him into a closet. He emerged 10 minutes later, let the bundle of handcuffs clatter to the floor and he was on his way to the big time.

His exploits made headlines across the nation as he successfully challenged some of the most celebrated prisons and insane asylums to keep him a prisoner. He escaped from straitjackets while hanging upside down high in the air, from buried coffins, jail cells, stocks and pillories, iron boilers riveted shut, a giant milk can filled with water and a mammoth football he had been laced into.

In his spare time, Houdini collected a fantastic library on spiritualism and magic apparatus used by famous magicians, old posters and handbills. His collection of Lincoln manuscripts was rated as one of the world's finest. In the 1920s Houdini wrote, produced and starred in adventure movies: "The Man From Beyond," "Terror Island" and "Haldane of the Secret Service." He performed most of his own perilous stunts including hanging over the edge of Niagara Falls.

Houdini also wrote books on magic: *The Unmasking of Robert Houdin, Miracle Mongers and Their Methods* and *Magical Rope Ties and Escapes.* His *A Magician Among the Spirits*, published in 1924, remains a classic expose of the tricks used by mediums to dupe their clients. Despite a friendship with Sir Arthur Conan Doyle, writer of Sherlock Holmes stories and a firm believer in communication with the spirit world, Houdini took particular delight in denouncing as frauds the world's leading spiritualist practitioners.

At the age of 52, Houdini was at the height of his popularity. A near perfect example of physical development, he was still capable of superhuman feats of strength and courage. He launched an exhausting coast to coast tour during the fall of 1926 that featured 2½ hour performances.

On October 10, Houdini suffered an accident while performing his famous Chinese water-torture act. As he was being lowered upside down into a container of water a small bone in his ankle was broken. Hopping on one foot, he finished his performance.

With his foot in a cast, Houdini stubbornly continued on the tour. Following a lecture on spiritualism at

McGill University in Montreal, a student presented him with a sketch he had drawn. Houdini invited the student to visit him backstage and make more sketches. The artist returned the next morning with two friends, one a college boxing star.

Houdini was lying on a couch in his dressing room, reading correspondence. The boxer asked him about a statement he had made that he could withstand the hardest blow to his abdomen. Houdini said that it was true and agreed to let him try it. As he was rising from the couch, the student punched him as hard as he could, three or four times, before the magician could tighten his muscles.

Houdini attributed the pain in his abdomen that grew increasingly worse as the day progressed to a torn muscle strand. Actually the blow had ruptured his appendix. As Houdini traveled by train to his next stop, Detroit, the pain grew more intense. But he refused to enter the hospital - the show must go on. Part way through his performance at the Garrick Theatre on October 24, he collapsed in the wings.

He was rushed to Grace Hospital. A team of surgeons operated and found an advanced case of peritonitis - a death sentence in the days before antibiotic drugs. Houdini mustered all his resources to battle the impossible odds. On the afternoon of October 31, he opened his eyes and muttered to his brother, "I'm tired of fighting; Guess this thing is going to get me," then closed his eyes forever.

Despite his long battle to expose spiritualism as a fraud, for 10 years on the anniversary of his death his wife and others held seances to communicate with his spirit. She gave that up in 1936 remarking "10 years is long enough to wait for any man." Other more steadfast believers continue to gather in darkened rooms each Halloween, hoping for a sign from the "world's greatest necromancer."

Bull Moose in Bay City

This 1912 postcard pokes fun at former president Theodore Roosevelt's
ill-fated "Bull Moose" movement and the Michigan Republican fiasco.

The chairman of the Michigan Republican convention gaveled and hollered for all he was worth to bring the meeting to order. Then another dignitary who thought he was chairman took his turn at the podium. Neither had any effect on the boisterous crowd of more than 1,000 delegates.

To the rear of the stage, "rump delegates" from Wayne County who had been turned away from the main entrance boosted one another through transom windows over a set of locked doors. The pandemonium worsened, fistfights broke out and a contingent of state police whaled into the melee. Finally, billy clubs accomplished what the gavel could not.

A scene from the 1988 Republican convention in Grand Rapids, featuring the tussle between George Bush and Pat Robertson? No, the year was 1912, the place the State Armory in Bay City and the candidates Theodore Roosevelt and William Howard Taft. And if you do not believe history repeats itself, read on.

After William McKinley's assassination in 1901, the "cowboy" vice president succeeded him to the White House. Teddy Roosevelt won election in his own right in 1904. After 7½ years of dynamic leadership featuring a broad array of progressive legislation, Roosevelt turned the presidency over to his friend Taft and left for an African safari. He returned in 1910 to find the "Grand Old Party" locked in factional strife, with the progressives battling a conservative element controlled by the old party bosses.

Taft, ponderous in appearance and more conservative than Roosevelt, had the support of the party machine. A group of liberal insurgents within the Republican Party organized the National Progressive Republican League in 1911. Under its banner, Roosevelt became a candidate for the Republican nomination, running against Taft, who he thought had violated his progressive principles. In Michigan, where the Republican Party had been born in 1854, the old-line political machine was strongly entrenched. Nevertheless, many Republicans backed the flamboyant Roosevelt.

Frank Knox of Sault Ste. Marie, a strong Roosevelt supporter, was chairman of the Republican State Central Committee. The committee met in Detroit in January 1912 and appointed Truman H. Newberry, who had been Roosevelt's secretary of the Navy, as temporary chairman of the state convention to be held in Bay City on April 9. The leadership of the Taft faction included U.S. Rep. Gerrit J. Diekema of Holland and Paul H. King of Dowagiac, secretary of the central committee.

In February, county caucuses were held to elect 1,312 delegates to the Bay City convention. They proved to be a preview of what was to come.

Because no specific laws governed caucuses then, whatever faction managed to gain control did pretty much as it wished. The Roosevelt forces won a fierce battle in Kent County, but in Calhoun County, rival delegates held two caucuses. The Wayne County caucus ended with both sides naming rosters of 192 delegates.

The pro-Roosevelt delegates left the Michigan Central Station in Detroit for Bay City at midnight the morning of the convention, ahead of the Taft delegates. But their cars got sidetracked, and the trains carrying the rival delegates raced past to arrive in Bay City well in advance.

Meanwhile, the Taft forces were usurping the power of the Central Committee. Secretary King called a special meeting, boycotted by Roosevelt backers, that approved all the contested Taft delegates and appointed a new pro-Taft Central Committee. They then stationed their men at the gates to the armory and only allowed pro-Taft delegates, who had been issued a special red ticket, to enter.

After the state police ended the ensuing riot, each side

elected its own six delegates to the national convention. At the Chicago convention on June 21, the Credentials Committee voted to seat the Taft delegates.

The day before, Roosevelt had ordered his supporters to bolt the convention. He later announced that in Michigan, Indiana and Kentucky, "the contest was marked by every species of fraud and violence on the part of our opponents."

Roosevelt supporters stayed on in Chicago to launch a progressive third party nicknamed the "Bull Moose" in his honor. Bandannas, a symbol of the plain working people, became its battle flag.

Roosevelt and his running mate, Hiram Johnson of California, did remarkably well for a third party during the November election. In fact, Roosevelt swept Michigan by a plurality of 62,340 votes and gathered more than 600,000 more votes nationally than Taft did.

The Democratic challenger, Woodrow Wilson, benefited, however, by the divided Republican vote to win an overwhelming electoral victory. Under Wilson's leadership, the Democrats enacted many of the reform measures advocated by the Progressive Party.

The Birth of the Michigan State Police

Michigan State Constabulary troopers pose before the Chevrolet Plant in Flint during World War I.

The summer of 1917 was a hot one on the Gogebic Iron Range. As the nation mobilized for the war declared against Germany on April 6, organizers for the Industrial Workers of the World, a militant labor union, had fanned widespread discontent among the iron miners. In early July they had shut down the Colby and Ironton Mines. The strike threatened to spread throughout the U.P. iron country, perhaps crippling the American war effort.

When Governor Albert E. Sleeper toured the mining region in mid-July, he found a tense situation. He repeatedly warned audiences that "the state would stand for no disorder." Yet Gogebic County Sheriff William Kellett seemed powerless to quell the mounting number of illegal disturbances. What's more, the Michigan National Guard had already been mobilized into the federal service to fight the Kaiser.

The situation worsened when a mob of miners formed in Bessemer and began marching east toward the Eureka Mine, intent on closing it by violence if necessary. On the evening of July 28, a special express train roared out of Lansing. The following morning it quietly pulled onto a siding in Bessemer. Fifty uniformed men filed out, unloaded their horses and equipment and within 15 minutes were cantering two abreast through the city's streets. Troop A of the Michigan State Constabulary had launched its first mission - to maintain law and order in the iron country.

The Michigan State Constabulary, forerunner of the Michigan State Police, had been created by the Legislature upon the recommendation of Governor Sleeper on April 10, 1917. Intended to be a small paramilitary unit, a crack force that could be speedily dispatched anywhere in the state, the constabulary was modeled after the Northwest Canadian Mounties and the only other state police forces previously in existence, those of Pennsylvania and New York.

Col. Roy C. Vandercook, veteran of the Spanish American War and former state adjutant general, was placed in charge of forming the constabulary. The total force was to number 200 men, including three mounted organizations and a motorized unit. Because of the limited time available for training, Vandercook handpicked seasoned veterans, including some who had fought Indians out West, and former college athletes for his elite force.

The main headquarters and the training camp were established on property loaned by the Michigan Agricultural College in East Lansing. By July 15, Vandercook had Troop A operational, barely in time for its first mission to the U.P. He personally commanded the unit dispatched to Bessemer.

As the troops fanned out on patrol that morning they found the city peaceful. Then Sheriff Kellett called Vandercook for help. He was powerless to disperse the mob of angry miners that had arrived at the Eureka Mine. Sixteen troopers galloped to the scene and charged the rioters with swinging billy clubs. The 300 miners broke and ran, ending the threat to the mine.

Two days later, Kellett learned of a mass meeting held by IWW agitators at the Bessemer Finnish Hall. Fearing another outbreak of violence, he requested Vandercook to send his entire force to handle the crowd. Instead, Vandercook sent only two troopers who stationed themselves outside the hall. The crowd, maddened by the fiery IWW oratory, surged toward the entrance but recoiled at the sight of the troopers. Then as the miners began sheepishly exiting the hall, the troopers ordered them home by various routes to prevent the formation of another mob.

The IWW organizers soon left for greener pastures and the trouble at Bessemer ended. Troop A remained on patrol in the U.P. throughout the winter of 1918. It responded to incidents in Negaunee and guarded the power dam at Menominee and the locks at Sault Ste. Marie against enemy sabotage.

Meanwhile, in East Lansing the rest of the constabulary was being recruited, trained and equipped. By August 15, 1917, the remaining three units were ready for action. Eight days later, 25 troopers were dispatched to the Port Huron tunnel to foil a suspected plot to dynamite it. They remained there on guard throughout the duration of the war.

Another contingent of the constabulary guarded the Detroit river front against infiltration by enemy saboteurs. Others patroled Flint, guarding automobile plants, rounding up slackers, as draft dodgers were then called, and investigating hoarded fuel supplies.

Rumors of a plot to blow up the Continental Motors Company plant and threats of a strike at the Linderman Wood Working Machinery plant brought a constabulary unit to Muskegon. At first fearful that the constabulary was there to break the strike, peaceful picketers at the Linderman plant later gratefully thanked the troopers for protecting them as well as the company's property.

The Michigan State Constabulary also found itself battling rum runners. While national prohibition did not go into effect until January 16, 1920, Michigan voted itself dry effective May 1, 1918. Wisconsin, Illinois and Ohio, however, remained wet. A lively trade in smuggled booze sprang up. Troopers patrolled the Wisconsin-Michigan border and stopped traffic for spot inspections for the illicit beverage. They also staged raids on notorious "blind pigs" located in Ramsey, Negaunee, Iron River, Stambaugh and Caspian.

In the lower peninsula, the highway leading from Toledo to Detroit proved a major pipeline for alcohol. Troopers apprehended smugglers who secreted booze in hot water bottles, aprons worn under maternity gowns, spare tires, hollow books, and ingenious tanks slung under vehicles. On September 8, 1918, a special detail

241

headed by Capt. C.E. Koch nabbed the infamous Billingsby brothers who had previously run an estimated 73 carloads of whiskey from Toledo to Detroit. The success of their trap, which featured an undercover agent and a mock bribe, would have made Elliot Ness green with envy.

Originally created as a temporary force to be disbanded at the war's end, the Michigan State Constabulary proved itself of such vital importance, particularly in fighting crime in rural areas, that in 1919 the State Legislature passed Act No. 26 which converted it into the Michigan State Police. The designation state trooper is a surviving vestige of the original cavalry-like organization.

Michigan State Constabulary troopers on patrol in the Upper Peninsula.

The Bath School Disaster

Wreckage of the Bath Consolidated School Building, the scene of Michigan's worst mass murder in 1927.

Monty Ellsworth remembered that smile until his dying day. He had rounded a corner in downtown Bath, hurrying to get rope to the scene of the disaster, when he passed his neighbor, Andrew Kehoe, in his Model T pickup. Kehoe waved and showed both sets of teeth in a wide grin, a malevolent smile, the smile of a maniac. Ellsworth did not realize it then, but it was Kehoe who had dynamited the Bath Consolidated School Building with 300 children inside - and he was not through yet.

Most of the residents of Bath, a Clinton County farm community, were mighty proud of the modern brick elementary schoolhouse that had opened in 1922. Instead of trudging miles to the one-room schoolhouses scattered throughout the district, pupils now rode school buses to the new facility.

Taxes, naturally, had gone up to pay for the structure and for other improvements, including purchase of a five-acre athletic field. The school millage had jumped from 12.26 mills in 1922 to 19.8 in 1926. That increase angered some, but none more than Kehoe. He now had to pay an annual school tax of $198 on his 80-acre farm and large home - and he had no children.

Kehoe had told his neighbors that if he were on the school board he would cut expenses. In 1924 the voters gave him a chance by electing him a trustee and the board appointed him treasurer.

Kehoe was a strange man. Born in 1872 on a farm near Tecumseh in Lenawee County, he was remembered by classmates and neighbors as someone who "didn't want to have anything to do with people who didn't do as he wanted them to."

Kehoe's mother had died when he was quite young and his father remarried. He did not get along with his stepmother. When he was 14, she returned from town one day and attempted to light the oil stove. Apparently someone had tampered with it and it blew up, setting her on fire. Kehoe watched her burn for a while before

244

throwing a pail of water on her, which spread the flames. The fire was extinguished before the house was destroyed, but Mrs. Kehoe died from her burns. Charges were never pressed against the teen-ager, but neighbors always felt that "he knew something about what was wrong with the stove."

Following graduation from Tecumseh High School, Kehoe studied electrical engineering at Michigan Agricultural College in East Lansing. He returned to Tecumseh and married Nellie Price, a former college classmate. The Kehoes attended the local Catholic church regularly until a new structure was built and he was assessed $400 to help pay for it. When the priest made a visit to find out why he no longer attended Mass, Kehoe ran him off his property.

Kehoe ultimately acquired the old family homestead and tried unsuccessfully to farm the 185 acres. It seems that he wasted too much time tinkering and trying to invent labor-saving gadgets rather than attending to business. He sold the homestead in 1919 and bought another farm near Bath where he continued his eccentric behavior. Neighbors found him eager to help them with mechanical projects and friendly providing they did not cross him. For example, he shot one neighbor's terrier when it barked at him.

He carried out his duties as school treasurer efficiently enough, but Kehoe made a troublesome board member. He nursed a personal vendetta against Emery Huyck, the school superintendent, and tried to ban him from board meetings. Whenever things did not go his way, Kehoe got angry and made a motion to adjourn the meeting.

In 1925, the Bath Township clerk died and for some reason the township board appointed Kehoe to serve in that position until the regular election the following spring. Kehoe ran for the office during that election but enough voters had heard about his actions on the school board to defeat him. That insult, in conjunction with rising taxes, a foreclosure notice on his farm and the strain of worrying about his sick wife apparently pushed him over the brink. He determined to take his revenge on the entire community in a way calculated to hurt the most.

He began traveling to Jackson and other outlets, purchasing large quantities of dynamite, ostensibly for blowing up stumps. Eventually he acquired nearly one ton of explosives. Neighbors were startled by a tremendous explosion precisely at midnight on New Year's Eve 1926. Kehoe explained he had experimented with a remote-control time detonating device.

Later that spring Kehoe worked out the final plans for his fiendish plot. On several evenings he loaded his pickup with dynamite, hid it behind some trap doors leading to the school's basement, drove home and then returned on foot to place charges throughout the structure.

It was a beautiful spring morning on May 18, 1927. At 9:45 a.m. many students were busy taking their final exams. Leona Gutekunst had gathered her primary class to the rear of their room for a story session and given in to their pleas to read them one additional story. Suddenly, with a tremendous blast, the entire brick wall crashed down on top of the vacant desks at the front of the room. She and her class escaped unhurt, but none of them remembered how.

Other classrooms were not so fortunate. The blast had disintegrated an entire wing of the school. Thirty-eight children and teachers lay dead or dying and scores more were trapped under the debris.

Kehoe had also rigged other charges that destroyed his own home, outbuildings and equipment at about the same time. He had murdered his wife two days before and now he headed for town in his truck loaded with explosives, rifle shells, bolts and other sharp bits of metal to finish his revenge.

When he got to town he was undoubtedly disappointed to see much of the school building still standing. Later the state police removed from the structure more than 400 pounds of dynamite that had failed to explode because Kehoe had used too weak a battery.

Thirty minutes after the blast, townspeople who were struggling to rescue those trapped under the ruins were jolted by another nearby explosion. Kehoe had blown himself and his vehicle up in the street, also killing Superintendent Huyck and three bystanders.

As reports of the Bath horror spread, rescue units sped from nearby communities. Governor Fred Green called on the people of Michigan to help the grief-stricken community. Senator James Couzens, a multimillionaire, donated money to rebuild the school. Thousands of Michigan schoolchildren gave their pennies for a memorial to the victims.

That memorial, a marble statue of a girl holding a cat, stands in the lobby of the Bath Community High School, a silent reminder of Michigan's worst mass murder.

The Bath Consolidated School Building before the blast.

When Every Bank in the State Closed for Eight Days

Governor William A. Comstock, who closed the state's banks in 1933.

Radio announcers startled the nation with the news on Tuesday morning, February 14, 1933. Michigan Governor William A. Comstock had closed every bank in the state for the next eight days - a bank holiday, he euphemistically called it.

Shocked Michiganians counted and recounted the bills in their wallets, nervously fingered pocket change and wondered how they were going to get by. Maybe their savings were gone forever?

Few had checking accounts, and the credit card had yet to be invented. Most paid for groceries with cash, counted out monthly house payments in currency, and it was not uncommon for a customer to walk into an automobile dealership and plunk down the full purchase price of a new car in good hard cash. Even employees of large corporations received real dollars and cents in pay envelopes.

It was the nadir of the Great Depression. Wild stock speculation on margin had triggered a rapidly declining economic spiral. American industry had misgauged the market, overextending itself, and now new plants lay idle across the land. One out of every four of the nation's breadwinners was out of work.

Lame-duck President Herbert Hoover worked feverishly to stem the financial panic. But he was philosophically unable to move with the boldness demanded by the crisis. The widely circulated rumor that president-elect Franklin D. Roosevelt intended to take the country off the gold standard spurred even more bank runs and hoarding of precious metals.

Michigan's automobile industry was particularly hard hit, and Detroit banks were in big trouble. A series of mergers had resulted in two dominant banking groups, the Guardian Detroit Union Group Inc. and the Detroit Bankers Group Inc. These holding companies had so intertwined their resources with other Michigan banks that the failure of one probably would bring the entire state's banking system crashing down.

An element of the Guardian Group, the Union Guardian Trust Company, was on the shakiest ground, chiefly because of overactive lending in real estate that plummeted in value because of the Depression. Hoover had established the Reconstruction Finance Corporation in 1932 to prop up the nation's banking system through emergency loans. The Union Guardian Trust Company promptly applied for and received loans of $15 million from the RFC.

Nevertheless, by early 1933 it was again in the red, with depositors' accounts and indebtedness well in excess of its available cash. What's more, it lacked the sound collateral legally required to receive another RFC loan. To circumvent that requirement, the Guardian Group transferred $88 million in collateral from member groups across the state to a newly formed Wolverine Mortgage Corporation. Then it reapplied for a matching loan.

RFC examiners, however, found those new assets to have a loan value of only $37 million. To help make up the difference, Edsel Ford agreed to freeze $7.5 million of Ford Motor Company deposits with the bank. The bankers also reduced the loan application to $50 million. But they still lacked approximately $6 million in collateral to get the loan.

Realizing a failure in Detroit might start a panic that could topple the entire country's banking structure, Hoover began negotiations. He met with Michigan Senators Arthur Vandenberg and James Couzens on February 9 to attempt to raise funds through private donors. But Couzens misinterpreted his strategy as a means to cause the RFC to make an illegal loan. Despite the fact he was from Detroit, on moral grounds Couzens stormed that if such a loan was made, he would "shout against it from the rooftops and on the floor of the Senate."

250

Hoover decided to make one last-ditch effort. He sent two Cabinet members to Detroit to appeal to Henry Ford for a $6 million loan. Cantankerous and headstrong, Ford not only angrily refused, but also withdrew his son's earlier pledge of $7.5 million. Ford thought it was the RFC's responsibility to keep banks from closing, not his.

Negotiations continued through Monday, a legal bank holiday, to no avail. After an urgent plea by the Detroit bankers, Comstock signed a proclamation at 1:30 a.m. Tuesday that closed all the state's banks for eight days.

Comstock's action precipitated a tidal wave of bank closings in other states. By March 4, inauguration day, virtually every bank in the nation had been closed or placed under restrictions. Roosevelt declared a four-day national bank holiday effective March 6. On March 9, Congress passed the Emergency Banking Relief Act which succeeded in checking the national panic. By its terms, federal examiners would decide which national banks were to be reopened or liquidated. The Michigan Legislature passed a similar act geared toward state banks on March 21.

Ultimately only 207 of Michigan's 436 state banks and trust companies were allowed to reopen. The liquidation of the remaining institutions was not completed until 1949. Depositors, however, eventually received nearly all of their funds. The Federal Banking Acts of 1933 and 1935 created a system which protects most depositors against a similar reoccurrence.

The Brown Bomber

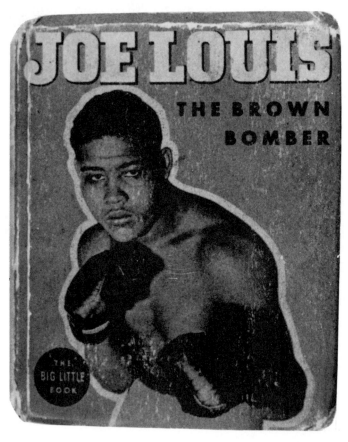

"Big-Little Book" biography of the "Brown Bomber," published in 1936.

They called him the Detroit Destroyer and the Michigan Mauler. They called him the Tan Menace, Dark Dynamite and Sepia Sniper. But it was as the Brown Bomber that Joe Louis would make ring history. Considered by many experts as "the best heavyweight boxer of all time," he provided inspiration and hope for Depression-era blacks and downtrodden whites as well. The Brown Bomber became an American folk hero.

Born Joseph Louis Barrows on May 13, 1914, he was the seventh of Munn and Lily Barrows' eight children. His boyhood was one of poverty and little schooling as his sharecropper family scratched a living from the red clay cotton fields near Lafayette, Alabama. When he was four his father died and three years later his mother remarried Patrick Brooks, a widower who also had eight children.

In 1926 Brooks moved the family to Detroit, lured there by the prospect of employment in the burgeoning automobile industry. Until the depression hit, they enjoyed relative prosperity. In the meantime, 12-year-old Joe enrolled in the third grade at Duffield Elementary School. A poor student, he never progressed beyond the sixth grade. Eventually, a kind teacher, thinking he might have a better future working with his hands, had him transferred to the Bronson Vocational School, where he studied cabinetmaking. In his spare time he supplemented the family income by working in a vegetable market and delivering ice. Lugging heavy blocks of ice up tenement stairs helped develop his magnificent physique.

His mother, a devout Baptist and the dominant parent, taught him dignity, honesty and self-respect. She also wanted her son to be more than a common laborer and allocated 50 cents a week out of their meager budget for violin lessons.

He hated violin lessons. When he was 16, a schoolmate introduced him to the world of the professional gymnasium. He began applying his violin money, unbeknownst to his mother, to boxing lessons. His sparring partners soon learned to respect his powerful punch, but he had a lot to learn about technique. Abbreviating his name to Joe Louis so that his family would not discover his secret, he fought his first amateur bout against Johnny Miler, a 1932 Olympic boxer. Miler knocked Louis down seven times in the first two rounds to win the match.

Despite that inauspicious beginning, he retained his shortened ring name. Louis knocked out his next three adversaries. Alternately boxing and working at the Ford River Rouge plant and other jobs, Louis battled his way to win the national Amateur Athletic Union light heavyweight title in April 1934. His overall amateur record of 50 wins in 54 fights included 43 knockouts.

Three months after winning the amateur title, Louis went professional as a heavyweight. Much of his continuing success stemmed from the excellent way in which he was managed. John Roxborough, a philanthropic black realtor, backed him and teamed him up with promoter Julian Black and trainer Jack Blackburn, a skilled veteran of the ring. Under Black's tutelage Louis added style to his murderous punching ability. Blackburn and Louis affectionately called each other "Chappie."

Just before the bell gonged for Louis' first professional fight against Jack Kracken on July 4, 1934, Blackburn told his protege, "Now, Chappie drive to de body with both hands and when he drop his guard jes hit him in de jaw." Louis followed his instructions and two minutes later Kracken lay stretched out on the canvas for the count of 10.

On May 7, 1935, a crowd at the Kalamazoo Armory watched the deadpan Louis knock out Gene Stanton in the third round, his 22nd in an unbroken string of victories. The month before he had plunked down a good share of his earnings to buy his mother a new home in Detroit.

Meanwhile, the legend of the Brown Bomber was growing. His next fight with the giant Italian and one-time heavyweight champion Primo Carnera took on international implications. Journalists linked the bout held in New York City on June 25 with the fact that Mussolini was preparing to invade Ethiopia. To America's delight, the black David felled the Italian Goliath in round six.

Next came King Levinsky, Max Baer, Paolino Uzcudum and Charley Retzlaff, all knocked out by Louis in less than four rounds. Louis accepted America's growing adulation humbly. He was taciturn but affable outside the ring, once inside there were no jokes, just jabs. Contrary to the unsavory exploits of the previous black heavyweight champion, Jack Johnson, Louis conducted a decorous social life, or as he revealed in the 1978 autobiography, at least a discrete one. Color barriers, including laws in some states prohibiting interracial prizefighting, rapidly fell before this clean-cut, all-American youth. Gene Kessler's 1936 "big little book" biography of Louis, intended for a juvenile audience, firmly placed the Brown Bomber in a special niche as a folk hero.

Then on June 19, 1936, Louis fought another match politically tied to the deteriorating situation in Europe - this time with one of Hitler's supermen, Max Schmeling. America gasped when Schmeling knocked Louis out in the 12th round. Louis characteristically offered no alibi for his first professional loss. "The man just whupped me," he told his mother.

But Louis bounced back to soundly "whup" his next 11 opponents, 10 by knockout. On June 22, 1937, he laid out James J. Braddock in Chicago in the eighth round to become heavyweight champion of the world. He removed the shadow left by his loss to Schmeling by a savage first-round knockout of the German during a rematch exactly one year later.

When World War II broke out, Louis volunteered for the army. For nearly four years he helped boost military morale by staging 96 exhibition matches before a total of two million soldiers.

On March 1, 1949, Louis retired as undefeated heavyweight champion. He tried a comeback in 1950, but Ezzard Charles won a 15-round decision. On October 26, 1951, Rocky Marciano ended Louis' ring career by knocking him out in the 8th round.

Louis had made a lot of money during his 12-year reign, but what did not go to his managers quickly slipped through his fingers. "I liked the good life," he later explained. Financial reverses, litigation with the IRS, drug addiction and marital problems marred his post-ring career. The man widely regarded as "the major black hero of his time" died of a heart attack in Las Vegas on April 12, 1981.

Michigan's Most Famous Dummy

Edgar Bergen and the "magnificent splinter," Charlie McCarthy, ca.
1950.

Eight-year-old Edgar Bergren sat in the kitchen of the family farmhouse near Decatur in Van Buren County watching his mother bake pies. Suddenly, a muffled old man's voice cried, "Hello, hello in there." Nellie Bergren opened the kitchen door, but no one was there. "I was sure I heard somebody" she mumbled. "So did I," said Edgar. Then from the oven came "Hello, Hello." Mrs. Bergren swung open the oven door and peered inside. At that her son broke out laughing and confessed, "I did it, Mother, I played a joke on you."

Little did Mrs. Bergren realize then, but her young prankster would parlay his special gift into a career as America's most famous ventriloquist.

Born in Chicago in 1903 to emigrants from Sweden, Bergren moved with his family to the Decatur area at the age of five. There he spent the next 11 years. Mrs. Arthur Howe, his fourth-grade teacher, later recalled that he demonstrated particular skill in art but not as an entertainer. But Harley Smith, a childhood chum, remembered the ventriloquist act he put on without a dummy at a school picnic held at Eagle Lake.

Bergren's first exposure to the world of entertainment came through a job at the Decatur opera house - sweeping the floor. But the proprietor, Gertrude Metzger, also let him pretend to play the player piano there during intermission. As a teenager, Bergren worked in the local onion fields. He bought a camera with the proceeds and used it to take pictures of departing doughboys which he sold to their families.

Bergren's father died soon after WW I began. Following the war, the family moved back to Chicago. There Bergren continued to hone his natural ability as a ventriloquist by studying a mail-order guide he had purchased for 25 cents. Whenever possible he also attended the performances of Harry Lester, a famous ventriloquist then playing in Chicago. Lester took the youth under his wing and gave him three months of free daily lessons.

Bergren was attending high school when he got the idea for Charlie McCarthy. One day he noticed a tough Irish newsboy standing on a street corner. Bergren sketched him and turned the drawing over to Theodore Mack, a skilled woodcarver. The wooden head Mack carved so delighted Bergren that he dubbed the dummy Charlie McCarthy, a Celtic version of the artisan's name.

One of Charlie's first feats was to help Bergren get out of high school. His grades were too low for graduation. But Charlie's witty repartee during school assemblies impressed faculty members and they gave him special tutoring which enabled him to graduate. After two years at Northwestern University, Bergren quit college to take his act on the Orpheum vaudeville circuit. About that time he dropped the "r" in his name to become Edgar Bergen.

For 10 years Bergen and McCarthy toured America and much of the world. When the popularity of vaudeville waned with the emergence of talking pictures, Bergen converted his routine into a night club act. In his most successful skit, called "The Operation," Charlie played the nervous patient and Bergen the inept doctor.

Bergen's big break came during a celebrity party in 1936. Charlie's saucy dialogue so impressed playwright Noel Coward that he got the team a booking on the Rudy Vallee radio show. Radio was an unlikely medium for a ventriloquist, but the act became an instant success.

In May 1937 Bergen got his own radio program with Chase & Sanborn Coffee as the sponsor. At a time when the radio was America's dominant source of entertainment, Bergen's show soon became one of the highest-rated programs on the airwaves. Bergen got a long list of prominent personalities to appear on his show for a merciless lampooning by McCarthy, the "magnificent splinter." Charlie asked portly Orson Welles, for example, "Why don't you release a blimp for active service?"

Bergen eventually added two other dummies to his act, bashful yokel Mortimer Snerd and Miss Effie Klinker, a man-hungry old maid. But Charlie remained his mainstay. The wisecracking 14-year-old puppet became a real personality to millions of Americans. Bergen wrote most of the jokes himself, but on stage he simply acted as a foil to Charlie, the real star.

Charlie, in fact, had his own luxurious dressing room, and his own stationery inscribed with his motto, "E Pluribus Mow 'Em Downus." Sixty percent of the act's voluminous mail came addressed to Charlie McCarthy. In the 1940s folks in Decatur campaigned to have a monument erected at the village limits, not to Bergen but to Charlie McCarthy.

Charlie's most memorable banter related to a mock feud of many years standing with W.C. Fields. Charlie would needle the great comedian with a question such as: "Is it true Mr. Fields that when you stood on the corner of Hollywood and Vine, 43 cars waited for your nose to change to green?" Fields replied: "Go away, you woodpecker's blue-plate, before I take my saw and pedicure your tootsies." So it went, to the delight of millions of listeners.

In 1938 Bergen and McCarthy starred in a lavish musical, "Goldwyn Follies" as well as Universal's "A Letter of Introduction." The Motion Picture Academy presented the team with a special wooden Oscar for their achievements that year. In 1939 they appeared with W.C. Fields in "You Can't Cheat an Honest Man." Foiled in his attempt to assassinate Charlie by feeding him to the lions, Fields' character, Larson E. Whipsnade, eventually cut a balloon's mooring rope to send the whole team aloft.

In 1941, at the height of his popularity, Bergen returned to Decatur to a hero's welcome. A crowd of

25,000 descended on the village for the festivities. Nearly twice that number of fans showed up when Bergen came to Decatur in 1948 as a special guest at the village's centennial celebration. When the mayor presented him with a key to the city Charlie quipped, "I can remember a time when Bergen wished he had a key to the Decatur jail." Bergen's final visit to the town of his youth came during the bicentennial celebration in 1976.

"The man who gave America a dummy for a national idol" died on September 30, 1978, following a performance at Caesar's Palace in Las Vegas. Charlie McCarthy now resides in the Smithsonian Institute.

BIBLIOGRAPHY

1. Pageant of the Sault

Bayliss, Joseph E., Estell L. and Quaife, Milo. *River of Destiny The Saint Marys.* Detroit, 1955.

Capp, Edward H. *The Story of Baw-a-ting Being the Annals of Sault Sainte Marie.* Sault Sainte Marie, Canada, 1904.

Fowle, Otto. *Sault Ste. Marie and Its Great Waterway.* N.Y., 1925.

Kellogg, Louise Phelps, ed. *Early Narratives of the Northwest 1634-1699.* N.Y., (1917).

"Saint-Lusson's Proces Verbal, June 14, 1671, "*Collections of the State Historical Society of Wisconsin.* Vol. XI (1888), p. 26.

Winsor, Justin. *The Pageant of Saint Lusson.* Cambridge, 1892.

2. The Griffin

Cunningham, Wilbur M. *Land of Four Flags.* Grand Rapids, (1961).

Dunbar, Willis F. *Michigan: A History of the Wolverine State.* Grand Rapids, (1965).

Hatcher, Harlan. *The Great Lakes.* London, 1944.

Havighurst, Walter. *The Great Lakes Reader.* London, (1969).

Pear, Lillian M. "Historical Houses in the Grosse Pointes," *Michigan History.* Vol. 42 No. 3 (September 1958), p. 353.

Quaife, Milo M. *Lake Michigan.* Indianapolis, (1944).

3. Indian Garden Beds

Blois, John T. *Gazetteer of the State of Michigan.* Detroit, 1838.

(Durant, Samuel). *History of Kalamazoo County, Michigan.* Philadelphia, 1880.

Fowler, Melvin L. "Middle Mississippian Agricultural Fields," *American Antiquity.* Vol. 34 No. 4 (October 1969), p. 365.

Fox, George. "The Prehistoric Garden Beds of Wisconsin and Michigan and the Fox Indians," *The Wisconsin Archeologist.* Vol. 40 No. 1 (March, 1959), p. 1.

Hinsdale, W.B. *Primitive Man in Michigan.* Ann Arbor, 1925.

Hubbard, Bela. *Memorials of a Half-Century.* New York, 1887.

(Kalamazoo) Ladies' Library Association. *Quarter Centennial Celebration of the Settlement of Kalamazoo, Michigan.* Kalamazoo, 1855.

Winsor, Justin. *Narrative and Critical History of America.* 8 Vols. Boston, 1889.

4. George Washington

Freeman, Douglas Southall. *George Washington, a Biography: Young Washington.* 2 Vols. N.Y., 1948.

Morris, Richard B. *Encyclopedia of American History.* N.Y., 1953.

Pare', George. *The Catholic Church in Detroit.* 1701-1888. Detroit, 1951.

Sawyer, Joseph Dillaway. *Washington.* 2 Vols. N.Y., 1927.

Webster, Mildred and Krause, Fred. *French Saint Joseph, Le Poste De La Riviere St. Joseph.* (Decatur, 1986).

5. Robert Rogers At Bloody Run

Armour, David, ed. *Treason? At Michilimackinac.* Mackinac Island, 1967.

Dunbar: *Michigan.*

Moore, Charles, ed. *The Gladwin Manuscripts.* Lansing, 1897.

Nevins, Allan, ed. *Ponteach or the Savages of America.* Chicago, 1914.

Peckham, Howard H. *Pontiac and the Indian Uprising.* Princeton, 1947.

6. Hull Surrenders Detroit

Catlin, George. *The Story of Detroit.* Revised Edition. Detroit, 1926.

Hatch, William Stanley. *A Chapter of the History of the War of 1812...* Cincinnati, 1872.

Parish, John C., ed. *The Robert Lucas Journal.* Iowa City, 1906.

Quaife, Milo, ed. *War on the Detroit.* Chicago, 1940.

Richardson, John. *War of 1812.* Toronto, 1902.

Tucker, Glenn. *Poltroons and Patriots.* 2 Vols. Indianapolis, (1954).

7. Treaty of Saginaw

Dustin, Fred. *The Saginaw Treaty of 1819...* Saginaw, 1919.

Dustin, Lawrence R., ed. *The Flint Journal Centennial Picture History of Flint.* (Flint, 1976).

Massie, Dennis. "Jacob Smith in the Saginaw Valley," *Michigan History.* Vol. 51 No. 2 (Summer 1967), p. 117.

Mills, James Cooke. *History of Saginaw County, Michigan.* 2 Vols. Saginaw, 1918.

Webber, William L. "Indian Cession of 1819, Made By The Treaty of Saginaw," *Michigan Pioneer Collections.* Vol. 26 (1894-95), p. 517.

Williams, Ephraim S. "The Treaty of Saginaw in the Year 1819," *Michigan Pioneer Collections.* Vol. 7 (1884), p. 262.

8. Bishop Baraga

Gregorich, Joseph. *The Apostle of the Chippewas.* Chicago, 1932.

Jamison, James K. *By Cross and Anchor.* Paterson, N.J., 1946.

Lambert, Bernard J. *Shepherd of the Wilderness.* L'Anse, 1967.

McGee, John W. *The Catholic Church in the Grand River Valley 1833-1950.* Grand Rapids, 1950.

Pare': *The Catholic Church in Detroit.*

Rezek, Antoine Ivan. *History of the Diocese of Sault Ste. Marie and Marquette.* 2 Vols. Houghton, 1906-07.

Sile Doty

Colburn, J.G., compiler. *The Life of Sile Doty.* Toledo,

1880. (Reprinted Detroit, 1948, with foreword by Randolph G. Adams).

"Michigan Greatest Thief," *Michigan Pioneer Collections.* Vol. 18 (1891), p. 676.

10. Singapore

Armstrong, Joe and Pahl, John. *River & Lake: A Sesquicentennial History of Allegan County, Michigan.* N.P., 1985.

Atlas of Allegan County, Michigan. Philadelphia, 1873.

Heath, Mary Francis. *Early Memories of Saugatuck.* Grand Rapids, 1946.

Lane, Kit. *Singapore: The Buried City.* Saugatuck, 1975.

Lorenz, Charles J. *The Early History of Saugatuck and Singapore, Michigan 1830-1840.* (Saugatuck, 1983).

Sheridan, James E. *Saugatuck Through the Years 1830-1980.* Detroit, 1982.

Starring, Charles. "Singapore: Michigan's Imaginary Pompeii," *Inland Seas.* Winter 1953, p. 231.

11. Caroline Kirkland

Kirkland, Caroline M. *A New Home or Life in the Clearings.* Edited by John Nerber. N.Y., (1953).

Osborne, William S. *Caroline M. Kirkland.* N.Y., (1972).

12. Willie Filley

Ballard, J.Z. *The Indian Captive or the Long Lost Jackson Boy.* Chicago, 1867.

De Land, Charles V. *De Land's History of Jackson County, Michigan.* Indianapolis, 1903.

13. Whitefish

Bayliss and Quaife: *River of Destiny.*

Beeson, Lewis, ed. "Kingston's Western Wanderings," *Michigan History.* Vol. 39 No. 2 (Sept. 1955), p. 282.

Davis, Marion M. "Three Islands," *Michigan History.* Vol. 12 No. 3 (July 1928), p. 513.

Erwin, Alice C. *"Nature Talks:" A Book of Days.* Harbor Springs, (1939).

Fowle, Otto. *Sault Ste. Marie and Its Great Waterway.* N.Y., 1925.

Hubbard, Bela "The Early Colonization of Detroit," *Michigan Pioneer Collections.* Vol. 1 (1874-76), p. 347.

Petersen, Eugene T. "Wildlife Conservation in Michigan," *Michigan History.* Vol. 44 No. 2 (June 1960), p. 129.

Stuart, L.G. "Letters of Lucius Lyon," *Michigan Pioneer Collections.* Vol. 27 (1896), p. 412.

Van Fleet, J.A. *Old and New Mackinac...* Ann Arbor, 1870.

Wood, Edwin O. *Historic Mackinac.* 2 Vols. N.Y., 1918.

14. Sugar Beets

Acts of the Legislature of the State of Michigan Passed At the Annual Session of 1839. Detroit, 1839.

Ball, John M. "Changes in Sugar Beet Production In Michigan, 1899-1958," *Papers of the Michigan Academy of Science, Arts and Letters.* Vol. XLV (1959), p. 137.

Blois: *Gazatteer.*

Butterfield, George Ernest. *Bay County Past and Present.* Bay City, (1957).

Dury, Wayne L. *White Pigeon. Prairie, Village, Township, Chief.* (Manchester, Tenn., 1987).

Henley, Ronald L. "Sweet Success... The Story of Michigan's Beet Sugar Industry." *Great Lakes Informant.* Series 3 No. 4.

History of St. Joseph County, Michigan. Philadelphia, 1877.

Howard, James. "European Agriculture," *Eighth Annual Report of the State Board of Agriculture of the State of Michigan.* Lansing, 1869, p. 207.

Kedzie, Frank S. "Sugar Production in Michigan," *Michigan History.* Vol. 16 (Summer 1932), p. 296.

Mills, James Cooke. *History of Saginaw County, Michigan.* 2 Vols. Saginaw, 1918.

State of Michigan. *Bureau of Labor Annual Reports.* Lansing, 1902-08.

Stuart, L.G., ed. "Letters of Lucius Lyon," *Michigan Pioneer Collections.* Vol. 27 (1896), p. 412.

Ure, Andrew. *A Dictionary of Arts, Manufactures and Mines.* N.Y., 1842.

15. First Railroads

Bonner, Richard I. *Memoirs of Lenawee County, Michigan.* 2 Vols. Madison, 1909.

Dodge, Mrs. Frank P. "Marking Terminus of Erie and Kalamazoo Railroad," *Michigan Pioneer Collections.* Vol. 38, (1912), p. 491.

Dunbar, Willis F. *All Aboard! A History of Railroads in Michigan.* Grand Rapids, (1969).

Frost, Clarence. "The Early Railroads of Southern Michigan," *Michigan Pioneer Collections.* Vol. 38, (1912), p. 498.

Hogaboam, James J. *The Bean Creek Valley.* Hudson, 1876.

Wood, Jerome James. *The Wilderness and the Rose.* Hudson, 1890.

16. Copper Country

Boyum, Burton. "Superior Copper and **Iron**," in *A Most Superior Land.* (Lansing, 1983).

Clarke, Robert E. "Notes From the Copper Region," *Harper's New Monthly Magazine.* No. 34 (March, 1853), p. 433 and No. 35 (April, 1853), p. 377.

Fuller, George N. *Geological Reports of Douglass Houghton.* Lansing, 1928.

Gates, William B. *Michigan Copper and Boston Dollars.* Cambridge, 1951.

History of the Upper Peninsula of Michigan. Chicago, 1883.

Jamison, James K. *This Ontonagon Country.* Ontonagon, 1938.

Lanman, Charles. *A Summer in the Wilderness.* N.Y., 1847.

Martin, John Bartlow. *Call It North Country.* N.Y., 1944.

Murdock, Angus. *Boom Copper.* N.Y., 1943.

17. Discovery of Iron

Brooks, T.B. *Geological Survey of Michigan: Upper Peninsula 1869-1873.* Vol. I. N.Y., 1873.

Cannon, George H. "The Life and Times of William A. Burt, of Mt. Vernon, Michigan," *Michigan Pioneer Collections.* Vol. V (1884), p. 115.

Dunbar: *Michigan.*

Everett, Philo M. "Recollections of the Early Explorations and Discovery of Iron Ore in Lake Superior," *Michigan Pioneer Collections.* Vol. XI (1888), p. 161.

Hatcher, Harlan. *A Century of Iron and Men.* Indianapolis, (1950).

History of the Upper Peninsula of Michigan. Chicago, 1883.

Holbrook, Stewart H. *Iron Brew.* N.Y., 1939.

Williams, Ralph D. *The Honorable Peter White.* Cleveland, (1905).

18. Fort Wilkins

Fisher, James. "Fort Wilkins," *Michigan History Magazine.* Vol. 29 No. 2 (April-June, 1945), p. 156.

Friggens, Thomas. "Fort Wilkins: Army Life on the Frontier," *Michigan History.* Vol. 61 No. 3 (Fall 1977), p. 221.

Frimodig, Mac. *The Fort Wilkins Story.* The Fort Wilkins Natural History Association, N.D.

Hamilton, Charles S. "Memoirs of the Mexican War," *Wisconsin Magazine of History.* Vol. XIV No. 1 (September 1930), p. 63.

19. Who Killed James Schoolcraft?

Bayliss and Quaife: *River of Destiny.*

Gilbert, Mrs. Angie Bingham. "The Story of John Tanner," *Michigan Pioneer Collections.* Vol. 38 (1921), p. 196.

Osborn, Chase S. and Stellanova. *Schoolcraft, Longfellow, Hiawatha.* Lancaster, Pennsylvania, 1942.

Steere, Joseph H. "Sketch of John Tanner, Known as the

'White Indian'," *Michigan Pioneer Collections.* Vol. 22 (1893), p. 246.

Williams: *Honorable Peter White.*

20. Thomas Edison

Ballentine, Caroline Farrand. "The True Story of Edison's Childhood and Boyhood," *Michigan History Magazine.* Vol. IV No. 1 (Jan. 1920), p. 168.

Dyer, Frank Lewis, Martin, Thomas Commerford and Meadowcroft, William Henry. *Edison: His Life and Inventions.* 2 Vols. N.Y., 1929.

Josephson, Matthew. *Edison.* N.Y., (1959).

McClure, J.B., ed. *Edison and His Inventions.* Chicago, 1879.

Stamps, Richard and Wright, Nancy. "Thomas Edison's Boyhood Years: A Puzzle," *Michigan History.* Vol. 70 No. 3 (May/June 1986), p. 36.

21. Dr. Alvin Chase

Chase, Alvin W. *Dr. Chase's Recipes; or Information For Everybody.* 10th ed. Ann Arbor, 1863.

_____ . *Dr. Chase's Third, Last and Complete Receipt Book...* Detroit, 1887.

Duff, Lela "Ann Arbor's Best Seller - Dr. Chase's Recipe Book," *Washtenaw Impressions.* Vol. 14, p. 14.

Historic Buildings Ann Arbor, Michigan. Ann Arbor Historic District Commission, 1977.

History of Washtenaw County, Michigan. Chicago, 1881.

22. Zachariah Chandler

Catton, Bruce. *The Coming Fury.* N.Y., 1961.

Dunbar: *Michigan.*

Faust, Patricia, ed. *Historical Times Illustrated Encyclopedia of the Civil War.* N.Y. (1986).

Harris, Wilmer C. *Public Life of Zachariah Chandler 1851-1875.* Lansing, 1917.

Statue of Zachariah Chandler... Proceedings in Statuary Hall... Washington, 1913.

Wilson, James G. & Fiske, John. *Appletons' Cyclopedia*

of *American Biography.* 6 Vols. N.Y., 1888.

Zachariah Chandler: An Outline Sketch of his Life and Public Services. Detroit, 1880.

23. Sarah Edmonds

Dannett, Sylvia, ed. *Noble Women of the North.* N.Y., 1959.

Edmonds, Sarah Emma. *Nurse and Spy in the Union Army.* Hartford, Connecticut, 1865.

Faust: *Civil War Encyclopedia.*

Fladeland, Betty. "Alias Franklin Thompson," *Michigan History.* Vol. XLII (1958), p. 345.

Harris, Fran. *Focus: Michigan Women 1701-1977.* Michigan Coordinating Committee of the National Commission on the Observance of Women's Year, 1977.

Millbrook, Mrs. Raymond H., ed. *Michigan Women in the Civil War.* Michigan Civil War Centennial Observance Commission Publication, 1963.

24. Robert Hendershot

Dodge, William Sumner. *Robert Henry Hendershot. or, the Brave Drummer Boy of the Rappahannoch.* Chicago, 1867.

Faust: *Encyclopedia of the Civil War.*

Foote, Corydon Edward and Hormel, Olive Deane. *With Sherman to the Sea.* N.Y., (1960).

Gerry, H.E. *Camp Fire Entertainment and True History of Robert Henry Hendershot...* Chicago, 1903.

History of the Nineteenth Regiment Massachusetts Volunteer Infantry. Salem, Mass., 1906.

Robertson, John. *Michigan In the War.* Lansing, 1882.

25. Beavers

Burt, William H. *The Mammals of Michigan.* Ann Arbor, 1946.

Dugmore, A. Radclyffe. *The Romance of the Beaver.* London, (1914).

Hubbard: *Memorials of a Half-Century.*

Johnson, Charles Eugene. "The Beaver in the Adirondacks: Its Economics and Natural History," *Roosevelt Wild Life Bulletin.* Vol. 4 No. 4 (July, 1927).

Johnson, Ida Amanda. *The Michigan Fur Trade.* Lansing, 1919.

Martin, Horace T. *Castorologia or the History and Traditions of the Canadian Beaver.* Montreal, 1892.

Mills, Enos A. *In Beaver World.* Boston, 1913.

26. James Redpath and Memorial Day

Douglas, George William. *The American Book of Days.* N.Y., 1948.

Faust: *Encyclopedia of the Civil War.*

Horner, Charles F. *The Life of James Redpath...* N.Y., (1926).

Wilson and Fiske: *Appleton's Cyclopedia of American Biography.*

27. Michigan Cavalrymen

Adams, James Truslow, ed. *Atlas of American History.* N.Y., 1943.

Annual Report of the Adjutant General of the State of Michigan for the Years 1865-66. Vol. 1. Lansing, 1866.

Faust: *Encyclopedia of the Civil War.*

Hebard, Grace Raymond and Brininstool, E.A. *The Bozeman Trail.* 2 Vols. Cleveland, 1922.

Livermore, Alfred S. *A Brief Sketch of the Life and Work of A.S. Livermore Against a Monster Evil.* Saginaw, 1890.

Miles, Nelson A. *Personal Recollections.* Chicago, 1897.

Record of Service of Michigan Volunteers in the Civil War. Vols. 31, 35, 36, 37. (Kalamazoo, 1903).

Robertson: *Michigan In the War.*

The War of the Rebellion: A Compilation of the Official Records of the Union and Confederate Armies. Series 1, Vol. XLVIII, Part 1. Washington, 1896.

28. Magnetic Mineral Springs

Furnas, J.C. *The Americans: A Social History of the United States 1587-1914.* N.Y., (1969).

Kennedy, Stiles. *The Magnetic and Mineral Springs of Michigan.* Wilmington, Del., 1872.

Michigan: A Guide to the Wolverine State. N.Y. (1941).

Moorman, J.J. *Mineral Springs of North America.* Philadelphia, 1873.

Rosentreter, Roger L. "Macomb County," *Michigan History.* Vol. 70 No. 4 (July/August 1986), p. 8.

Tucker, Willard D. *Gratiot County, Michigan. Historical, Biographical, Statistical.* Saginaw, 1913.

Tuttle, Charles, Richard, ed., *General History of the State of Michigan.* Detroit, 1874.

Walton, George E. *The Mineral Springs of the United States and Canada.* N.Y., 1873.

29. Will Carleton

Carleton, Will. *Farm Ballads.* N.Y., 1873.

Corning, A. Elwood. *Will Carleton, A Biographical Study.* N.Y., 1917.

Douglas: *American Book of Days.*

Finney, Byron A. "Reminiscences of Will Carleton," *Michigan History.* Vol. VI No. 4 (1922), p. 583.

Special Day Programs for Michigan. Lansing, 1923.

30. Bidwell Brothers

Bidwell, Austin. *From Wall Street to Newgate Via the Primrose Way.* Hartford, Conn., 1895.

Bidwell, George. *Forging His Chains.* Hartford, Conn., 1888.

Baxter, Albert. *History of the City of Grand Rapids.* N.Y., 1891.

Kyes, Alice Prescott. *Romance of Muskegon.* Muskegon, 1974.

31. Centennial Celebration

McCabe, James D. *The Illustrated History of the Centennial Exhibition.* Philadelphia, (1876).

Mc Cracken, S.B., ed. *Michigan and the Centennial.* Detroit, 1876.

Visitors' Guide to the Centennial Exhibition and Philadelphia. Philadelphia, (1876).

32. Warren Sheffield's Velocipedes

Cutler, H.G., ed. *History of St. Joseph County, Michigan*. 2 Vols. Chicago, N.D.

Fairbanks, Morse & Co. Railroad Department Catalogue. Chicago, 1899.

Massie, Larry B. and Schmitt, Peter. *Kalamazoo: The Place Behind the Product*. Woodland Hills, California, 1981.

Pioneers in Industry. The Story of Fairbanks, Morse & Co. 1830-1945. Chicago, 1945.

Sheffield Car Company Mining Cars and Wheels Catalogue No. 7. N.P., N.D.

_____ . *Self-Propelling and Other Cars for the Maintenance of Way Department Catalog*. N.P., N.D.

Sheffield Velocipede Car Co. Catalog. Buffalo, 1887.

33. Julia Moore

Blair, Walter, ed. *The Sweet Singer of Michigan*. Chicago, 1928.

Greenly, A.H. "The Sweet Singer of Michigan Bibliographically Considered," *Papers of the Bibliographical Society of America*. Vol. 39 (Second Quarter), 1945, p. 91.

Moore, Julia. *The Sentimental Song Book*. N.Y., (1912).

Nye, Bill. *Bill Nye and Boomerang*. Chicago, 1881.

34. Wreck of the Alpena

Bowen, Dana Thomas. *Shipwrecks of the Lakes*. Daytona Beach, Florida, 1952.

Elliot, James L. *Red Stacks Over the Horizon*. Grand Rapids, (1967).

Eyler, Jonathan. *Muskegon County, Harbor of Promise*. Northridge, Cal., (1986).

Hill, Jno. C. *Memorial of the Rev. Farel Hart and His Wife Lottie Davis Hart*. Syracuse, N.Y., 1881.

Kyes: *Romance of Muskegon*.

(Mansfield, James). *History of the Great Lakes*. 2 Vols. Chicago, 1899.

35. Buffalo Bones

Barnett, LeRoy. "Buffalo Bones in Detroit," *Detroit in Perspective.* Vol. 2 No. 2 (Winter 1975), p. 89.

Cook, James H. *Fifty Years on the Old Frontier.* New Haven, 1923.

Dary, David A. *The Buffalo Book.* Chicago, (1974).

Gard, Wayne. *The Great Buffalo Hunt.* N.Y., 1960.

Towne, Arthur E. *Old Prairie Days.* Otsego, (1941).

36. Pioneer Christmas

Diaries, Archives and Regional History Collections Western Michigan University.

Douglas: *American Book of Days.*

Engle, W.A. *Poems.* Chicago, (1883).

Rowland, O.W. *A History of Van Buren County, Michigan.* 2 Vols. Chicago, 1912.

37. Battle Creek Sanitarium

Hill, W.B. *Experiences of a Pioneer Minister of Minnesota.* Minneapolis, 1892.

Kellogg, John Harvey. *The Battle Creek Sanitarium System.* Battle Creek, 1908.

Massie, Larry B. and Schmitt, Peter J. *Battle Creek: The Place Behind the Product.* Woodland Hills, (1984).

Schwarz, Richard W. *John Harvey Kellogg, M.D.* Nashville, Tennessee, (1970).

38. Dr. Feodor Protar

Price, Antje. "F. Protar, The Heaven Sent Friend," *The Journal of Beaver Island History.* Vol. 1. N.P., 1976.

_____. "Protar Revisited," *The Journal of Beaver Island History.* Vol. 2. N.P., 1980.

_____. "The Real Protar." *The Journal of Beaver Island History.* Vol. 3. N.P., 1988.

39. Silver and Gold

Bryan, William J. *The First Battle.* Chicago, 1896.

Cook, Sherwin, Lawrence. *Torchlight Parade: Our Presidential Pageant.* N.Y., 1929.

Gardner, Washington, ed. *Michigan Legislative Manual and Official Directory for the Years 1897-98.* Lansing, 1897.

Herrick, Genevieve Forbes and Origen, John. *The Life of William Jennings Bryan.* Chicago, (1925).

Lindsay, Vachel. *Collected Poems.* N.Y., 1925.

Morris: *Encyclopedia of American History.*

Reimann, Lewis C. *Incredible Seney.* (Ann Arbor, 1953).

Starring, Charles R. "Hazen S. Pingree: Another Forgotten Eagle," *Michigan History.* Vol. 32 No. 2 (June 1948), p. 129.

Stone, Irving. *They Also Ran.* N.Y., 1944.

40. Round Oak Stoves

Glover, Lowell H. *A Twentieth Century History of Cass County, Michigan.* Chicago, 1906.

Greeley, Roger E., ed. *Ingersoll: Immortal Infidel.* Buffalo, (1977).

Norton, Willard A., *Directory of Dowagiac, Cassopolis...* St. Joseph, 1899.

Round Oak Stove Company Catalog. N.P., 1925.

Vanderburg, Berenice E. *A Dowagiac Collection.* Berrien Springs, (1982).

41. Merry Oldsmobile

Edmonds, J.P. *Early Lansing History.* Lansing, 1944.

Forbes, B.C. & Foster, O.D. *Automotive Giants of America.* N.Y., 1926.

Hand Book of Gasoline Automobiles. Association of Licensed Automobile Manufacturers. N.Y., 1906.

Kestenbaum, Justin L. *Out of a Wilderness: An Illustrated History of Greater Lansing.* Woodland Hills, California, 1981.

May, George S. *A Most Unique Machine.* Grand Rapids, 1975.

————. *R.E. Olds: Auto Industry Pioneer.* Grand Rapids, 1977.

Partridge, Bellamy. *Fill'er Up! The Story of Fifty Years of Motoring.* N.Y., 1952.

Rae, John B. *The American Automobile: A Brief History.* Chicago, 1965.

42. Dr. James M. Peebles

Barrett, J.O. *The Spiritual Pilgrim.* Boston, 1871.

Lowe, Berenice Bryant. *Tales of Battle Creek.* (Battle Creek, 1976).

Massie and Schmitt: *Battle Creek.*

Nostrums and Quackery. 2 Vols. Chicago, 1912 and 1921.

Peebles, James M. *Seers of the Ages.* Chicago, 1903.

43. "Hurry Up" Yost

Behee, John. *Fielding Yost's Legacy to the University of Michigan.* Ann Arbor, 1971.

Douglas: *American Book of Days.*

"History of American Football" *Michigan vs Harvard Program.* Nov. 9, 1929, p. 77.

Lawton, J. Fred. *"Hurry Up" Yost in Story and Song.* Ann Arbor, 1947.

Perry, Will. *The Wolverines A Story of Michigan Football.* Huntsville, Ala., (1974).

Sagendorph, Kent. *Michigan The Story of The University.* New York, 1948.

Yost, Fielding H. *Football for Player and Spectator.* Ann Arbor, 1905.

44. Booker T. Washington in Cass County

Bergman, Peter M. *The Chronological History of the Negro in America.* N.Y., (1969).

Fields, Harold B. "Free Negroes In Cass County Before the Civil War," *Michigan History.* Vol. 44 No. 4 (December 1960), p. 375.

Glover: *A Twentieth Century History of Cass County.*

Standard Atlas of Cass County, Michigan. Chicago, 1896.

Washington, Booker T. "Two Generations Under Freedom, *Outlook*, February 7, 1903, p. 293.

45. Jackson Bicyclists

Murphey, Claude C. *Around the United States By Bicycle.* Detroit, *1906.*

46. Harry Houdini

Christopher, Milbourne. *Houdini: The Untold Story.* N.Y., (1969).

Gresham, William Lindsay. *Houdini: The Man Who Walked Through Walls.* N.Y., (1959).

Kellock, Harold. *Houdini.* N.Y., (1928).

47. Bull Moose

Campbell, Alice Porter. "Bull Moose Movement in Michigan". *Michigan History.* Vol. 25 (1941), p. 34

Dunbar: *Michigan.*

Morris: *Encyclopedia of U.S. History.*

Russell, Thomas H., ed. *The Political Battle of 1912.* N.P., (1912).

48. State Constabulary

A History of the Michigan State Constabulary. Detroit, 1919.

Olander, Oscar G. *Michigan State Police: A Twenty-Five Year History.* N.P., 1942.

Smith, Bruce. *The State Police, Organization and Administration.* N.Y., 1925.

49. Bath Disaster

Ellsworth, M.J. *The Bath School Disaster.* N.P.. (1927).

Parker, Grant. "Disaster In Bath", *Michigan History.* Vol. 65 No. 3 (May/June 1981), p. 12.

50. Bank Holiday

Barnard, Harry. *Independent Man: The Life of Senator James Couzens.* N.Y., (1958).

Dunbar: *Michigan.*

Morris: *Encyclopedia of American History.*

Russel, Robert R. *A History of the American Economic System.* N.Y., (1964).

Sullivan, Lawrence. *Prelude to Panic: The Story of the Bank Holiday.* Washington, (1936).

51. Joe Louis

Current Biography. N.Y., 1940.

Durant, John and Rice, Edward. *Come Out Fighting.* N.Y., (1946).

Kessler, Gene. *Joe Louis: The Brown Bomber.* Racine, Wisconsin, (1936).

Louis, Joe and Rust, Edna. *Joe Louis: My Life.* N.Y., (1978).

McGowen, Deane. "Joe Louis, 66, Heavyweight King Who Reigned 12 Years, Is Dead," *New York Times.* 13 April 1981, p. 1.

52. Edgar Bergen

Berges, Marshall "Charlie McCarthy and Friend," *Modern Maturity.* June/July 1978, p. 13.

Current Biography. N.Y., 1945.

Everson, William K. *The Art of W.C. Fields.* N.Y., (1967).

Fields, Ronald J. *W.C. Fields By Himself.* Englewood Cliffs, (1973).

Howland, Catherine, ed. *Scrapbook History of Decatur, Michigan and Vicinity.* N.P., 1976.

Local History Vertical Files. Webster Library. Decatur, Michigan.

INDEX

Author. (Photo courtesy Kalamazoo Gazette, Rick Campbell, photographer)

Larry B. Massie is a Michigan product and proud of it. He was born in Grand Rapids and grew up in Allegan. Following a tour in Viet Nam as a U.S. Army paratrooper, he worked as a telephone lineman, construction laborer, bartender, and in a pickle factory before earning three degrees in history from Western Michigan University.

He honed his research skills during an eight-year position with the W.M.U. Archives and Regional History Collection. He left in 1983, to launch a career as a free-lance historian specializing in the heritage of the state he loves. An avid book collector, he lives with his wife and workmate Priscilla, and their 25,000-volume library, in a one-room schoolhouse nestled in the Allegan State Forest. Sons, Adam, Wallie, and Larry Jr., as well as a border collie named Maggie, and Jiggs, a huge saffron-colored feline, insure there is never a dull moment.

PLEASE RETURN TO:

avery
COLOR STUDIOS

P.O. Box 308
Marquette MI 49855

CALL TOLL FREE
1-800-722-9925

Your complete shipping address:

_____

_____

_____

_____

Fold, Staple, Affix Stamp and Mail

_____

_____

_____

_____

avery
COLOR STUDIOS

P.O. Box 308
Marquette MI 49855